W9-BAH-873

ARMED AND DANGEROUS

ARMED AND DANGEROUS

The Hunt for One of America's Most Wanted Criminals

WILLIAM QUEEN AND DOUGLAS CENTURY

RANDOM HOUSE NEW YORK

Copyright © 2007 by Carolina Queen, Inc.

Published in the United States by Random House, an imprint of The Random House
Publishing Group, a division of Random House, Inc., New York.

RANDOM HOUSE and colophon are registered trademarks of Random House, Inc.

978-1-4000-6577-6

Library of Congress Cataloging-in-Publication Data
Queen, William.
Armed and dangerous: the hunt for one of America's most wanted criminals /
William Queen and Douglas Century.
    p.   cm.
ISBN 978-1-4000-6577-6
1. Queen, William.   2. United States. Bureau of Alcohol, Tobacco, and Firearms—
Officials and employees—Biography.   3. Stephens, Mark.   4. Fugitives from justice—
United States.   5. Criminals—United States.   I. Century, Douglas.   II. Title.
HV8144.B87Q84   2007
364.1'77092—dc22   2007005428

Printed in the United States of America on acid-free paper

www.atrandom.com

2 4 6 8 9 7 5 3 1

FIRST EDITION

All photographs are from the collection of William Queen

Book design by Casey Hampton

DEDICATED TO THE TEAM

THAT STOOD WITH ME ON THAT MOUNTAINTOP

ARMED AND DANGEROUS

One

Everyone called him the mountain man. They said he was the most dangerous, gun-crazy renegade seen in the hills and valleys of Southern California since the days of the Wild West outlaws. The local police departments and sheriffs' offices all said it would be next to impossible for any cop or federal agent to bring him down alive from his mountaintop hideout.

In April 1986, when I first caught wind of Mark Stephens—this "mountain man" terrorizing the Inland Empire communities (those in Riverside and San Bernardino counties)—I was only in my third year as a special agent with the Department of the Treasury's Bureau of Alcohol, Tobacco and Firearms. But I'd been a law enforcement officer for over a decade, and I'd made my bones as a local cop in North Carolina and as a federal border patrol agent before becoming an ATF agent—I'd certainly heard my share of war stories. Some so-called badass or another was always being touted as the hardest, most cold-blooded criminal in the county, the scariest dude to make the most-wanted lists. *I seen this guy whip a dozen cops,* other cops would tell you. *This guy, he ain't gonna be taken alive. He's crazy. If you try to get cuffs on him, he'll kill you.* Ninety-five percent of the times when I confronted these so-called tough guys, all the fight instantly drained out of them. Their ruthlessness turned out to be nothing more than a front, an actor's persona. When I cornered them, they folded up, dropped their guns, and surrendered without so much as a peep.

But there are those few criminals out there who are righteously *bad.* Guys who won't give up without a fight. And when you do decide to confront them, you'd better be ready to fight for your life.

Mark Stephens was one such criminal. Stephens was the real McCoy, the most brazen and fearless criminal I encountered in my early years with ATF. He proved to be equal parts gunman, mountain man, drug trafficker, and out-and-out thug.

Mark Stephens was a paradox for a criminal investigator. He didn't fit the stereotype: He didn't come from the wrong side of the tracks and wasn't abused as a kid; he wasn't semiliterate or lacking in career opportunities. His parents were well-educated, fairly affluent people who lived in an upscale neighborhood in Rancho Cucamonga, a city of nearly one hundred thousand, located under the majestic San Gabriel mountain range in the Inland Empire, thirty-seven miles east of my ATF desk in downtown Los Angeles.

Sometimes the path to a criminal personality can't be easily explained; the factors that determine one's character defy reason. Mark Stephens wasn't a typical bully, the kind of person who seemed to get emotional gratification from picking on the weak. It didn't make any difference to him whether you were male or female, old or young, black or white—if you stood in his way, he was going to hurt you. Stephens was a man who had no conscience when it came to taking what he wanted by force. And he'd learned early on in life that hurting people was the way to get what he wanted. The intelligent man locked inside of him may have known that violence was wrong, that he had an uncontrollable problem. But violence physically possessed him; it was an overwhelming force he simply couldn't rein in. He understood that it would land him in prison one day, and prison wasn't an option for Stephens. So he decided to separate himself from society—literally. He headed for the hills, disappearing into the vast, impenetrable San Bernardino Mountains.

Stephens put together a basic plan. He would live off the land. He'd grow marijuana in prodigious quantities, smoke as much of it as he wanted, and sell the excess kilos when he needed cash to buy firearms and explosives. He would be as self-sufficient as a human being could be; he wouldn't depend on any friends or family. The only people he would interact with would be the small network of low-level drug dealers he would keep in check with constant threats. His only daily companions would be the wild animals in the mountains. It was a near-perfect plan for a lone wolf determined to live outside the borders of civilized society.

I'm something of a lone wolf myself. It's a character trait that has worked to my advantage during investigations. Special agents for the Bureau of Alcohol, Tobacco and Firearms are often charged with the task of operating as a one-man law enforcement agency. Our mandate is primarily to enforce violations in firearms and explosives laws, but our jurisdiction in this area encompasses a wide range of criminal types—narcotics traffickers, traditional organized-crime families, outlaw bike gangs, inner-city gangs such as the Bloods and the Crips, and anti-government and hate groups such as the neo-Nazis and Aryan Nations.

Special agents with ATF have two basic options. They can forge a smooth, relatively hassle-free investigator's career by focusing on background work, running errands for the administrators, and picking up what we call "adoptive cases"—that is, bringing in federal resources and manpower to investigations that were initiated and completed by local law enforcement. Or they can take my career path. Always pushing into overdrive. Making cases against *real* bad guys. Putting themselves in harm's way by getting right in the line of fire and, if necessary, going undercover to get the most violent criminals off the street.

Throughout my ATF career, often to the dismay of my supervisors, I took that "put your life on the line" attitude to the limit. In dozens of cases, I went undercover to infiltrate armed organizations such as the Skinheads and the Aryan Nations—

and most notably, in the late nineties, near the end of my ATF stint, when I penetrated the Mongols outlaw motorcycle gang in a landmark two-and-a-half-year investigation. During that case, playing the part of a biker badass named Billy St. John, I achieved something nearly unthinkable for a federal agent: I became a "patched-in" member of the club and eventually rose to the position of treasurer and vice president of the Mongols' San Fernando Valley chapter.

Going deep undercover or running and gunning in the streets always fueled me. I thrived on that high-risk energy. Call it an adrenaline addiction or sheer machismo, but I felt like that was where my investigative talents were best utilized. I wanted to be out on the firing line. Wearing a coat and tie behind my desk at headquarters, typing up the stream of official reports and memoranda, I felt like a fish out of water. My place was in the street, down in the trenches, chewing the same dirt with the state and local cops.

In early 1986 I was a thirty-seven-year-old recently married special agent. My wife at the time and I lived in a peaceful bedroom community called Corona and I commuted to ATF Metro Group headquarters in downtown Los Angeles. Since I lived in the Inland Empire, it was only natural that I'd start poking around the various police departments and sheriffs' offices, expressing an interest in what criminal cases they saw brewing. I was looking for the real bad guys. I always tried to do it in as low-key a manner as I could. Locals often don't appreciate the unsolicited attention of special agents from the FBI, DEA, or ATF. They see the feds as being overpaid and self-serving, sweeping in to take the glory of a promising investigation away from blue-collar cops.

I've always found that interagency rivalries are most pronounced at a senior management level, where a lot of publicity is at stake; a few headline-grabbing cases can bump an administrator up the Bureau hierarchy pretty damn quick. For rank-and-file ATF agents like me, developing close working relationships with local law enforcement was essential. Many of us started out our careers as local patrolmen, so we knew what made cops tick and could appreciate the nitty-gritty of police work. Though we carried federal badges and credentials, we talked, thought, and did our jobs like cops.

In my day-to-day routine, I would pop in at different agencies around Southern California and make contacts with detectives and patrolmen, the behind-the-scenes guys working dangerous assignments in narcotics and gang units. I told them I was the kind of guy who kept my ear to the pavement. I left them my card and let them know that if they needed federal help, I was the guy at the ATF Metro Group in L.A. to call. If the local guys needed help, I was there. I never stepped in where I wasn't wanted. And it was completely up to me if I took on a case or not.

In every department I visited, I'd always ask who was the biggest threat in the area in terms of gun crimes. Early in 1986, over and over again, I kept hearing the name Mark Stephens. He either had outstanding warrants or was a prime suspect in felonies in nearly every community from Pomona to San Bernardino.

The boys in the detective division at the Montclair Police Department first briefed me on Stephens. For some months I'd been working closely on a case with a young Montclair detective named Bill Kendrick. In his late twenties and sandy-haired, Kendrick was a straight-shooting, no-nonsense cop; I could quickly see that we shared the same love of street work and the same distaste for hunkering down behind an IBM Selectric to keep our bosses satisfied with the requisite paper trail.

One afternoon over coffee in the squad room, Bill Kendrick began telling me stories about Stephens that sounded so far-fetched, so outlandish, I wondered if he was planning on soon leaving the underpaid cop world to take a stab at a career as a Hollywood screenwriter.

Mark Stephens was unlike any other bad guy Kendrick had encountered. From his hideout in the hills, he had built up a small arsenal of machine guns and hand grenades. His acts of violence were well documented, but eyewitnesses were nonexistent. No one would dare come forward and give testimony against him. Over the years, with his hair-trigger temper, Stephens had built a foolproof shield, scaring the shit out of everyone who'd witnessed him in action.

I asked Kendrick the obvious question: "Why's nobody going up in the hills to take him down?"

Kendrick let out a laugh without cracking a smile. "You don't understand, Queen," he said. "When I say this son of a bitch lives up in the hills, I mean he lives up in the *hills*."

He got a map to show me the general vicinity. I immediately understood the scope of the challenge: Stephens had picked a virtually inaccessible area in the San Bernardino Mountains, so high up in the badlands that no one had been able to get near him. The Montclair Police Department didn't have a lot of solid intel on his exact whereabouts, but they did know that the camp was located somewhere north of Rancho Cucamonga and approximately ten miles west of El Cajon Pass. Stephens had been living like a hermit in the mountains for about five years, tending to his marijuana crops and coming down from his hideout only to sell his dope and commit acts of violence in the communities of the Inland Empire. His patterns of movement were completely unpredictable.

I began mulling over the facts I would need to obtain a federal warrant. Growing marijuana on federal land was enough, of course, but I wanted more. My bosses wouldn't move unless there was irrefutable evidence that Stephens posed a public-safety risk. I asked Bill Kendrick about the known acts of gun-related violence.

Kendrick said that Stephens had been involved in countless unsolved shootings. He never came down from the mountain without one of his machine guns or semiautomatic pistols, and he wouldn't hesitate to blast people who crossed him or to spray gunfire indiscriminately into homes and businesses. Most knew his reputation; few dared to cross him. He had managed to intimidate a network of criminal associates into doing what he wanted, which was selling his dope and getting him more firearms. At any one time, Kendrick told me, Stephens had four or five dealers in various towns who sold marijuana for him. All the dealers were scared to death—Stephens had left them no choice. He might as well have said, *Work for me, or I'll have to fucking kill you.*

Kendrick's briefing had me hooked. I told him I was going to swing by the Berdoo sheriff's office to see what they had in their Mark Stephens file. As I got up to leave, Kendrick shook my hand and said he was glad to have me on the case. Then he laughed.

"This guy's right up your alley, Queen."

"How's that?"

"He's as wild as they come. When he shoots up a place, the motherfucker does it with a machine gun."

I initially thought I was only going to pitch in on a local investigation that was already up and running. The Stephens case was atypical. In fact, there was no case to speak of. I didn't realize that I was going to end up taking the lead investigative role, developing my own operational plan from scratch and ultimately going against Stephens man-to-man. I didn't realize that the cat-and-mouse game was going to consume me, all but taking over my life.

After leaving Bill Kendrick, I shot over to the San Bernardino sheriff's office and reviewed their confidential files. Putting together some kind of psychological profile was essential if I was going to make a serious effort to take Stephens down. What I found most fascinating about him was his self-awareness. He apparently knew he had a mental disorder. But if he was a psychopath, he was an extremely intelligent one, the kind who knew he couldn't deal with other people. He seemed to know that he had homicidal tendencies, but he also enjoyed the power they gave him. He was always ready to deal with other people in the most violent manner. He'd realized very early on in life that the working world held no place for him; it was impossible for him to hold down a nine-to-five. Instead, he started every day armed to the teeth, prepared to resolve any situation with bloodshed. By now most of the tax-paying citizens in the middle-class neighborhoods Stephens frequented knew his reputation. He'd terrorized them with his hand grenades, machine guns, and bare fists. Everyone knew that before Stephens left town for his hideout in the hills, somebody almost invariably would be hurt—possibly killed.

Stephens was fearless. He was in extremely good shape, a little over six feet and a rock-hard two hundred pounds of muscle. I was astonished when I read the file accounts of his lightning escapes up to his place in the mountains. In a matter of hours, he could complete a treacherous climb that would take even an athletic and trained lawman a day and a half.

The more I learned about Mark Stephens, the more one thing became clear: Time was running out. Stephens's acts of violence were becoming more brazen. It was only a matter of months, perhaps weeks, before he ended up killing someone.

Stephens's name was on most-wanted lists throughout the Inland Empire. By any measure, his apprehension should have been a top law enforcement priority. Why, then, was no one putting together a viable operational plan for his arrest? Why had all previous attempts to apprehend him failed?

As far as I could see, two factors made Stephens nearly impossible to catch. The first was simple geography. He'd chosen to make his home in some of the most inaccessible and rugged terrain in the United States. Although it lay just a few hours' drive east of L.A., that mountain wilderness might as well be some impenetrable forest in Central America or New Guinea. The only trails leading to his camp were stamped down by mountain lions, deer, goats, and rabbits. The hills were covered with dense chaparral, and the mountain passes would prove challenging to even an expert climber.

I had been up in the San Bernardino Mountains many times; I knew the difficulty of the terrain. There were places where you had to crawl on your hands and knees to get through the vegetation, places where you had to use ropes to rappel down a steep cliff face. If you slipped and fell off the cliff, no rescue team was going to find your remains. The coyotes and vultures would take care of you first.

Multiple agencies wanted to slap the cuffs on Stephens, but in the past five years none had been able to catch him out of his backyard. Two of the Southern California elite extraction units —the SWAT teams of the San Bernardino Sheriff's Department and the Fontana Police Department—had made well-coordinated attempts to apprehend him, using sophisticated surveillance and dozens of officers. They'd even attempted to fly helicopters up to the mountain man's retreat. Each time Stephens eluded them.

The second reason Stephens was such a difficult target was because he was a true survivalist. He barely needed any contact with the civilized world. He lived in a canvas tent without electricity or running water, like some wild character out of the West's frontier days. But at the same time, he managed to keep one foot in the twentieth century, maintaining his major marijuana-growing operation and indulging his obsession with state-of-the-art weaponry.

I saw few viable avenues of attack. My gut instinct told me that Stephens's drug business was key. Could it be his one weakness? It involved contact with other people. Maybe one of his dealers could provide me with an in. However erratic his movements, Stephens would need to leave his mountain hideout and connect with his street-level dealers fairly regularly in order to keep his operation running smoothly. If I could somehow plot out his movements, I might have a shot at catching him away from his hideout, where he had every advantage.

I wasn't sure how I'd do it, but from the beginning I was confident that I could bring this heavily armed renegade into custody alive. Looking back, I don't know why I thought I could do what a lot of good cops and SWAT teams couldn't. I'm not so arrogant as to think I'm some kind of supercop. But I did know one thing: Stephens's survivalist plan for evading law enforcement played perfectly into my personal background. I had developed skills from my pre–law enforcement years that would give me a leg up against him.

Survivalist techniques were something I mastered at a pretty young age. Straight out of high school, I joined the army and did a tour in Vietnam. I volunteered for Special Forces and served with C Company, 3rd Battalion, 11th Special Forces Group. We often had no choice but to use our own wits in the dense wilderness. During training at Fort Bragg, we spent days in the Uwharrie National Forest of North Carolina, practicing techniques of silently creeping up on the enemy, moving through vegetation quietly, fording streams, and camouflaging ourselves to evade the enemy's sight lines. Backwoods living came naturally to me. I'd soaked it up as a kid, decades before my Green Beret training. Back in the fifties, it was the way we were raised in rural North Carolina. Almost before we learned to read and write, my twin brother and I learned how to hunt and fish and live for days in the woods.

I realized that as long as Mark Stephens could take refuge in that mountain forest, he would have the upper hand. He would remain supremely confident, knowing he could outsmart, outrun, or outgun almost any city, state, or federal cop who came looking for him. They could come with helicopters and telescopic surveillance, but they wouldn't find traces of his footprints in those mountain passes. He owned the terrain as much as any black bear or coyote.

The one thing Stephens probably never imagined was that he might run up against a Special Forces wood-hook country boy from North Carolina like me. He never figured he'd find himself getting stalked by a good ol' boy who was comfortable crawling on his hands and knees down some overgrown deer trail. Stephens was ready for anything twentieth-century law enforcement could throw at him, but he wasn't expecting to come face-to-face with a North Carolina throwback, a cop who could get just as down and dirty, just as backwoods and Daniel Boone, as he could.

Two

I was born into the hill country of western North Carolina and led a real rustic backwoods childhood. I was delivered in my parents' small wood-frame house with a tin roof, five minutes ahead of my twin brother. Our sister was a year and a half older.

My father, Bill Queen, Sr., handed down a legacy of more than his name. My dad was a lifelong lawman and the sole reason I became a federal agent myself. He was a tough country boy who grew up in and around Rutherford County, who early on learned how to hunt and fish and would often leave home for days at a time, stalking and killing game to help make ends meet. Hunting wasn't a game for my dad—it was survival.

When he graduated from high school, World War II was in full swing, so he joined the navy's UDT, or underwater demolitions team, an elite outfit that was the forerunner to the SEALs. In 1945 he was on a ship, getting ready to slip into Japan to blow up defenses meant to repel Allied forces, when the second atomic bomb was dropped on Nagasaki. The war was over in a few days, and my dad was on his way back to Rutherford County.

But a taste of the outside world hit a switch with my old man, and Rutherford County was no longer big enough for the country boy. He left behind his hillbilly roots to head for the big-city excitement of Washington, D.C. I guess he was hooked on the adrenaline rush he had found in serving with UDT and needed that excitement full-time. He found it in a career as a cop with the Washington, D.C., park police.

My dad couldn't quite slip the country, though. He met and married my mother, a stunning redhead from West Virginia who had also fled the country in search of the city life. They didn't plan on kids, but a short time following their marriage, my sister was born. Not long after that, my brother and I were born. A family was the last thing our parents were looking to start. They both wanted to enjoy a life of freedom and excitement, and being tied down with kids wasn't part of their plan. My mother had gone back to Rutherford County to deliver me and my brother, but she had no intention of staying there. We all went to Washington, D.C., for a short time, but the family life wasn't going to work out for Mr. and Mrs. Bill Queen.

While they worked in the nation's capital, my parents left me and my brother and sister to live in Rutherford County with our aunt Johnnie in a little country home we called Up-on-the-Hill. We didn't see much of Mom and Dad for the next few years, only on special occasions, like birthdays or Christmas. As we grew into rambunctious kids, the life of hunting and fishing that our dad had known so well captivated me and my brother, too. Our dad, who was born with a restless streak and was looking for even more out of life than being a park policeman in D.C., lucked out when the feds began searching for a few good men to chase the likes of Snuffy Smith and his bootlegging buddies around the South. Dad soon found himself back in North Carolina, not as a patrol cop but as what was then called a "revenuer"—a latter-day agent for the Bureau of Prohibition of Eliot Ness fame.

The agency would undergo a myriad of name changes before I found my path there as an adult: from the Bureau of Prohibition, it morphed into the Bureau of Alcohol, Tobacco and Tax (ATT); then to ATU, or Alcohol Tax Unit; then to ATF, or Alcohol, Tobacco and Firearms. Today the agency is formally known as the Bureau of Alcohol, Tobacco, Firearms and Explosives. The job, however, stayed largely unchanged from the Roaring Twenties days of Eliot Ness to the early sixties, when revenuers chased bootleggers mainly in the southeastern United States.

On the way to my dad's first fed assignment in Greensboro, North Carolina, he and my mom stopped by Rutherford County and picked up us kids and Aunt Johnnie and brought us down to Greensboro with him.

At the time I didn't think much of it when my dad and his fed buddies would stop at the house, break out their Thompson submachine guns and plan raids. For a six-year-old boy, it was just a part of life. Growing up around guns and fast cars was a way of life for our family, and the influence of the early country days would stay with me forever. Back in the Depression, when my father was in grade school, he was given a gun, shown how to shoot it properly, and then expected to go out and make good use of it. I suppose he felt his boys would naturally take up skills without any training at all. During the summers, our parents sent us kids back to Rutherford County from Greensboro so we could spend time with our relatives there. When my twin and I were eleven years old, Dad gave us our first gun—a .22-caliber semiautomatic rifle. We picked up the skills quickly, and rabbits and birds around our area of operation found life a bit more hazardous. We were good shots with that .22. It didn't matter how far away a can was; if we could see it, we'd ding it. Most people who shot targets out of the air would do it with a shotgun, but my brother and I mastered it with the rifle. Predictably, things started to get a bit out of hand. Boredom set in, and plinking cans didn't cut it anymore: My brother and I began shooting cans off each other's heads.

When that got old, one of us would sit in a swinging chair (which we called a glider), and while he swung, the other would shoot tin cans off his head with the cherished .22. It was during one of these William Tell sessions that the shit hit the fan. One of our neighbors looked out her window and watched in horror at the sight of me taking aim at my brother's head. *Bam!* The shot rang out, and she ran from her house screaming for Aunt Johnnie. "Lawd have mercy! Johnnie Sue, *Lawdy, Lawd*! Johnnie Sue, come quick!"

Our aunt ran from the house to see what tragedy possibly could have befallen us. My brother and I stopped to see what had happened. The neighbor grabbed Aunt Johnnie, all out of breath: "They gonna kill each other, they gonna kill each other." Aunt Johnnie was at a loss. "Them boys!" the neighbor said, pointing at us. "They shootin' cans off each other's fool heads!"

Now, I knew I wasn't gonna shoot my brother and that he wasn't gonna shoot me, but you would think we had already killed each other by the way my aunt reacted. "Lawd have mercy!" Aunt Johnnie shouted. I'm not sure how many times I heard Aunt Johnnie shout that as she stomped her way toward us. "Just wait till your daddy hears about this," she said, glowering. "Now gimme that damn gun."

Life Up-on-the-Hill was never quite as carefree after that.

We didn't have a lot of money growing up. By 1956 there were two sets of twins in the family, making five of us. My twin brother, Jimmy, and I spent a lot of time camping out for entertainment. We had learned to fish and hunt early, and we'd learned that killing animals was not a sport but something you did for food. If you caught fish, you either cleaned them and ate them or threw them back. I had friends who were also into trapping and survivalist-type activities, only we didn't call it survivalist training, we called it hard-core camping. When I was twelve years old it was nothing to go into the woods for several days at a time. Our parents didn't worry that we were going to be abducted or murdered. It wasn't a problem back in those simpler times.

Although I grew up with a great deal of respect for law enforcement, given my father's choice of careers, I didn't always act in accordance with the law. If you talked with people I went to high school with, they'd tell you that Bill Queen, Jr., was voted the student most likely to end up in prison. I was always into trouble. Not mean or violent stuff, just stupid crap. It was a good thing my dad knew all the law enforcement people in the Greensboro area, or I probably wouldn't have made it into the army. It takes some people a little longer to grow up, I guess.

One day when I was in high school, I heard my dad talking about a boxcar load of Budweiser beer being shipped to a distributor in Greensboro without the required tax being paid on it. As it turned out, the Budweiser corporation found that it was going to cost more to have the beer shipped back than it would to forfeit the beer for destruction. The problem of getting rid of the beer fell to ATF, since back then beer was canned in steel without pop-tops. ATF found an abandoned well where the owner gave permission for trucks to come in and dump the load of cans. The trouble was, my dad never should have been discussing the plan of dumping a boxcar load of Budweiser in front of his son, who knew where the well was. I could hardly believe my ears—enough beer to furnish me and my friends for the next couple of years. It seemed like a gift from heaven.

The day after the Budweiser was dumped, I grabbed Eddie Rider—one of my beer-guzzling buddies—and a rope and bucket, then headed to the well. I tied the rope around my waist, and down in the well I went. In a matter of minutes, Eddie and I had hauled up all the beer we could put in his mother's car. Party time. Around Ragsdale High School, we were now kind of folk heroes, at least among the drinking crowd. But in less than a couple of days, the principal at Ragsdale had me and my accomplice in his office. I thought we were going to spend the rest of our school days in federal custody for contributing to the delinquency of the Ragsdale student body. Lucky for me, the authorities deemed it more appropriate that I hand over what was left of the beer, and I wasn't charged with anything. We were ordered to spend the rest of the academic year picking up trash at school for punishment, though.

I played sports in school, mostly football and baseball. But cars were my main passion. My friends were always interested in my dad's work and especially in the souped-up cars he drove. In high school, I got the itch to race stock cars someday. North Carolina is the mecca of NASCAR and home to a bucketload of famous drivers. Richard Petty lived only a few miles away from us. We didn't toss around the Petty name because of their racing fame but because my dad took his G-ride there to get tuned up and set up for road racing. Others such as Junior Johnson and Wendell Scott were road-racing adversaries of the revenuers around North Carolina and Virginia.

Later, when I was a police officer in High Point, I was bitten by the racing bug and sold a beautiful 1967 Corvette coupe so I could buy my first race car—a 1965 Mercury Comet—from a local racing legend named Mickey York who ran limited late-model racing, mainly at the Caraway Speedway in Asheboro, North Carolina. About the same time, I was working part-time for Bill Blair Racing Engines in High Point, where we built engines for people like Richard Childress and Skip Manning. I would buy my racing fuel from the Pettys and talk with Lee Petty about my old man bringing his G-cars down there to get set up. Lee told me that he always did a good job for my old man, but they always did just a little better for the bootleggers who brought their cars in. Lee and Richard Petty would laugh about the car-chase stories between the revenuers and the bootleggers, most of the time involving my dad. Lee and Richard were always good to me and some of the finest people I would ever meet.

Back in 1968, the war in Vietnam was going strong. Within two weeks of graduating from high school, caught up in a surge of teenage patriotism, my twin brother and I were at Fort Bragg, North Carolina, reporting for boot camp. I would find my way back to Bragg for Special Forces training later on. My brother would make it back to serve with the 82nd Airborne Division.

I was eighteen and thought I could save the world. I did one tour in Vietnam running patrols from 1970 to 1971, almost always humping my favorite weapon, an M60 machine gun. I went in-country in Cam Ranh Bay and saw action at Da Nang. I worked the I Corps area of operations, which ran from Da Nang to the DMZ.

I was lucky I got my ass out alive.

After my discharge from the army, all I wanted to do was to become a police officer and then, possibly, an ATF agent. Since my dad was an ATF agent, it seemed like a career path I was destined to take. I had watched him for years, and his job was a constant source of excitement for me. He also seemed to have the respect of all the law enforcement officers in North Carolina, from the local cops to the state guys. His jurisdiction ran from coast to coast, and he always drove the fastest cars available to law enforcement.

I started off my career as a local city cop in High Point, North Carolina. As I became more experienced in local law enforcement, I realized more and more that the feds were often held in higher esteem than the locals. I constantly heard stories about what the feds were able to take on, cases that were beyond the reach of my city cop job. I also respected them more because the feds all needed college degrees before they could even be considered for the job. I decided to go back to school, get that college degree, and become a fed. I enrolled at Guilford College in Greensboro, and in 1980 I received my undergraduate degree with a major in administration of justice.

Being a fed wasn't an ego thing for me. I really wanted to make a difference; I wanted to put the hard-core bad guys in jail. As a cop, I was brimming over with enthusiasm and soon found I had some talent when it came to taking on the bad guys on the street. I developed a knack for undercover work and often asked for those risky assignments. I would pick out the especially dangerous groups or people to go after. In my heart, I knew there were no criminals or criminal organizations that were bigger than the feds. I didn't care how dangerous or how elusive they seemed to be; if I got them in my sights, they were going down.

Three

I t wasn't long after I started pursing Mark Stephens in April 1986 that word reached me of a particularly chilling incident that had taken place a few days earlier in the town of Fontana. As expected, no witnesses were willing to come forward and go on record against Stephens, but we caught a big investigative break by getting the victim himself to work as a confidential informant for ATF.

They say a cop is only as good as his network of informants. I was lucky to start developing a strong group of confidential informants (otherwise known as CIs), men and women who'd had firsthand encounters with Stephens and were courageous enough to cooperate with my investigation.

Tony M. was one of the first CIs on the Stephens case. He was a rough Inland Empire character who would become a key source of intel for me. So was Tony's wife, Joanne, who was young and blond and the mother of their two small children; I met with her to hear about what had happened in Fontana. Still trembling, pale with fear, she sat down with me and detailed the terrifying rampage she'd just survived.

For some time Tony had been selling marijuana on a consignment basis for Mark Stephens. Like a lot of dealers, he wasn't very precise in his bookkeeping methods. Despite Stephens's propensity for violence, Tony had made the mistake of messing up his end of the finances. As I was to find over and over again in this investigation, the one thing Stephens didn't take lightly was when people owed him money. His grass dealers weren't on a particular schedule, and neither was he. Instructions were simple. Stephens fronted a dealer the dope; the dealer sold it; and when Stephens got the urge to get the money owed him, he'd show up on the dealer's doorstep. He expected his dealers to be available to him whenever he decided to do business, impractical as that might seem.

On that warm April evening, Stephens came down from the hills looking for Tony. Tony wasn't home, and his wife didn't know when he'd be back. After riding around Fontana and the surrounding areas for over an hour, Stephens must have been boiling, growing angrier by the second. He wanted his money.

He wanted Tony to know that putting him on the back burner was a bad mistake. He decided to drive back to Tony's house one more time. When he rounded the corner near the house, Tony's car still wasn't back in the driveway.

Stephens exploded. He slammed on the brakes in front of Tony's house, tires shrieking, drawing the attention of Joanne. By now Stephens had seemingly lost control of himself. He reached over to the passenger seat, picked up his MAC-10 submachine gun, and slid the bolt to the rear.

A MAC-10 (or Military Armament Corporation Model 10) is a fearsome weapon, a blowback-operated 9mm submachine gun capable of delivering up to a thousand rounds per minute. The gun's compactness and high rate of fire make it a favorite tool of terror for drug dealers nationwide. I'd seen firsthand what a MAC-10 could do to the human body. More often than not, I saw the grisly evidence on a slab in the medical examiner's office.

MAC-10 in hand, Stephens got out of his car. Joanne watched from her window, peeking through the curtains as he approached her car. Without warning, Stephens let go with a thirty-round burst of machine-gun fire, riddling the side of her vehicle. When the smoke cleared, Stephens's fury was still intense.

Shooting up the car didn't appear to relieve his frustrations. He turned toward the house and saw Joanne standing at the window, horrified by what she'd witnessed. She was locked in place, couldn't move an inch. Her heart was pounding, and she later told me she'd felt like she was in a waking nightmare. Very calmly and deliberately, Stephens went back to his car, retrieved another thirty-round magazine, and popped it in his machine gun. After reloading, Stephens locked his cold stare on Joanne.

"What happened, Mommy?" one of her small children asked.

Joanne snapped back to consciousness. Somehow she found the composure to grab her children, pulling them to the floor a split second before Stephens began firing the next thirty-round burst into the house.

The gunfire was deafening. The windows came crashing in. Wood furniture shattered. Plaster walls ripped open.

While glass and debris flew through the living room, Joanne dragged her children into the kitchen, barely escaping the 9mm bullets tearing through the walls beside her. She curled up by the refrigerator, using her body to shield the children from Stephens's fury. She held her children tight until the bullets stopped. In the few seconds of calm, her terror intensified. She huddled over her children and imagined Stephens loading up his next magazine, preparing to storm inside the house to murder her and the children in cold blood.

Joanne made a sudden dash for the hallway phone and dialed 911. Her voice was almost too hysterical to be understood by the operator. Over and over, Joanne screamed, "Help me! Help me! He's gonna kill us!"

Having emptied the two magazines he'd carried down from the mountain, Stephens returned to his car. He may have been a homicidal maniac, but he wasn't stupid. He knew that the black-and-whites would be swarming to the scene any minute. But he'd made his point; he knew the next time he came looking for Tony M., that motherfucker would have his cash.

Stephens started the ignition. Time to get out of Fontana, ditch the car, and slip back into the hills on foot.

Joanne later told me that she'd caught a glimpse of Mark Stephens's face through the shattered windows. He'd been laughing as he peeled out of her driveway.

All April, as I drove the freeways and city streets of the Inland Empire, I would find myself gazing at the San Bernardino Mountains, thinking about Stephens. From the 10 freeway, I could see the area where Stephens was camping out, somewhere high in the wilderness above the Cajon Pass.

The Cajon Pass, separating the San Gabriel Mountains from the San Bernardino Mountains, played a memorable role in the history of the Old West. The Cajon used to be the only gateway through the mountains negotiable by wagon trains. It was the point at which all the old frontier-era trails converged: the Mojave, Santa Fe, Mormon, and Spanish trails. The path was well traveled by Indians, trappers, explorers, and scouts on their way to the San Bernardino Valley. The region is still dotted with ghost towns, abandoned mining camps, and old cowboy graveyards. As I looked up, I thought about the countless outlaws and gunmen who'd taken refuge in the wilderness there over the years.

I wondered what this modern-day gunman was doing at that

moment. Watering his marijuana crop? Cleaning one of his ma-chine guns? As I drove out to San Bernardino, the closer I came to Stephens's camp, the more intense my feelings grew. I'd chased down scores of bad guys in my years as a cop and a fed-eral agent, and I'd always tried to depersonalize the work. I locked up bad guys because it was my job, not because of some emotional agenda or grudge.

But something about Mark Stephens was different. After the Fontana incident, he'd gotten under my skin, even though he was just a vague image in my head at that point. I didn't even know what Stephens looked like. No mug shot was on file with any of the local police departments, and the physical descrip-tions we had were bare-bones: white male in his mid-thirties, bearded, about six feet tall, and powerfully muscled.

Time and again as I cruised the 10 in my Mustang, I heard myself muttering in the wind. It was always the same phrase. *I want this guy; I want this guy bad.*

It was the kids who got me. Putting children in harm's way was off the charts, even by the code of hardened criminals. A guy like Tony M. was different. Tony was a full-grown man who had made the conscious choice to get mixed up in the drug game—he *knew* what the rules were if he screwed around with Stephens's money. He knew that extreme violence was part of the drug game. But most drug dealers wouldn't involve innocent kids. What kind of animal would unload a full clip of MAC-10 gunfire at a defenseless woman and her children?

During that spring, my wife, Mary, and I were talking about

starting a family. (A few years later, we were blessed with the birth of our two sons.) During my confidential interview with Joanne, I jotted her words in my notebook and kept up a tough exterior. But inside, her words stabbed me like an ice pick. I couldn't get the images out of my head; at home with Mary, I'd lie awake in the middle of the night, thinking about how narrowly that little boy and girl had come to being shot and killed.

This case was personal. In the wake of the Fontana incident, I made a promise to myself. I vowed that, however many hours it took, however many administrative roadblocks the ATF bosses might put in my way, I wasn't going to rest until I brought Mark Stephens down off that mountain in handcuffs.

But doubts gnawed at me. Could I get him in time? Could I lock him up before he committed cold-blooded murder?

The first thing I needed to do was understand why the previous attempts to get Stephens had failed.

A week after the Fontana incident, I talked to the cops at the Fontana Police Department about their aborted operation on the mountain. A few months earlier, finally fed up with the way Stephens kept coming into their town and threatening the public with his guns, the police had authorized its SWAT team to make a run at Stephens's camp. The operational plan was to head up the mountain on foot and try to catch Stephens by surprise. From aerial surveillance, they gained a rough idea where he was likely to be camping out.

The team decided to follow the creek bed right to Stephens's camp. However, what sounded feasible on paper proved much more difficult in the field. The team had failed to grasp the difficulty of the terrain or how far the hike to the hideout really was. Although they'd started early in the day, by the time they got close to his camp, the sun was setting. In the mountain darkness, the SWAT team started getting jumpy. They knew Stephens was well armed and wouldn't hesitate to shoot at cops. Worse, they were in his backyard, and he had all the strategic advantages. It was bad news all around. The team leader made a smart decision in backing out: He ordered his guys down the mountain rather than into an ambush. No arrest is ever worth the loss of a cop's life. Fontana SWAT didn't make any more attempts. They'd decided it was too dangerous to go into Stephens's backyard.

Around noon on April 14, I hooked up with the guys from the San Bernardino Sheriff's Department SWAT team. Berdoo SWAT had more intel to relay about Stephens's excursions in their jurisdiction. They'd done several recon missions into the hills to try to locate Stephens over the past few months. They had made numerous helicopter flybys in an attempt to locate Stephens's camp, but it wasn't until they hooked up with Steve Kilgore, a veteran investigator from the U.S. Forest Service, that they were able to pinpoint the camp's general vicinity.

Stephens treated the San Bernardino National Forest like his personal playground. Even if you did get the drop on him, he had a mind-bogglingly vast territory to escape into. Covering more than eight hundred thousand acres, the San Bernardino National Forest has two main divisions: the San Bernardino Mountains, on the easternmost Transverse Range; and the San Jacinto and Santa Rosa Mountains, on the northernmost Peninsular Range. The elevations range from 2,000 to 11,502 feet. According to Steve Kilgore's assessment, Stephens's camp had been carefully located in one of the highest, most inaccessible areas in the forest.

After those flyovers, Berdoo came to the conclusion that an air insertion—a helicopter drop of SWAT team members—on the mountaintop at the same altitude as Stephens's camp would be the way to go. But the altitude and rough terrain made for a dangerous combination, especially in the blazing bone-dry summer heat; fast-moving forest fires were an ever-present risk.

It was an early-morning mission, and the airdrop part of the operation went off without a hitch. The helicopter pilot set the SWAT team down on the other side of the mountain. However, just like the Fontana SWAT team, the Berdoo boys soon realized how difficult the terrain really was. The brush was often impenetrable, and the trek turned out to be more than Berdoo had bargained for. By the time the SWAT team was in position to see Stephens's camp, it was getting dark. They managed to get closer to him than Fontana had; they were approximately a thousand yards out when they spotted Stephens with their binoculars. He was tending his marijuana plants, watering and pruning, with a machine gun hanging casually around his neck. They watched him meticulously working his weed crop for some time. But Berdoo realized it was far too dangerous to try to continue; it was a near-suicidal proposition. Like Fontana before them, they chose to back out of the mission rather than fight this guy on his terms. Berdoo SWAT's assessment was that it would be much better to try to catch Mark Stephens during one of his forays out of the hills, but to date they hadn't been able to do that.

It was ominous, listening to Berdoo SWAT describing Stephens as a grave and increasing threat to the citizens of San Bernardino County, telling me that going into his backyard wouldn't be just dangerous, it would be damn near impossible.

The intel from the San Bernardino police got my motor racing. It was obvious that the local cops were up to their butts in Stephens's mayhem and needed ATF help. Machine guns, growing dope on U.S. government land, and an ongoing campaign of violence made Stephens a target that ATF was designed to take down.

In general, local law enforcement agencies around the country have more respect for ATF than they do for any other federal agency—especially the FBI, which has the reputation of coming at the locals with an overbearing and arrogant attitude. When ATF agents work in conjunction with locals, however, the local agencies tend to defer to the fact that we're a federal agency. For the most part, they have no problem with our taking the lead in an investigation.

But I never liked to push too hard by insisting that a case be prosecuted in the U.S. federal court system. To me, a prosecution in state court was as good as a federal one. If a successful prosecution got a bad guy behind bars, that was enough for me. In fact, if the advantage went with the state or locals, then that was the way I liked to play it. That didn't always sit well with my administrators at ATF. Some of my bosses, of course, wanted to make federal cases that enhanced their own stature within the federal bureaucracy.

I had heard enough talk about other agencies trying to get Mark Stephens. Berdoo and Fontana had taken their shot at Stephens and missed—it was time for us to take a crack. I took my intelligence back to the office and put it into a 3270 report of incident (or "ROI"), the standard ATF paper trail when conducting a criminal investigation.

My group supervisor at the ATF Metro Group was Mort Jacobson, who had recently transferred to Los Angeles from New York City. He was in his early forties, tall, somewhere around six-four, and skinny. He was somewhat lacking in interpersonal skills, and his style with the rank and file was loud and bullying. His attitude seemed to be "don't rock the boat" whenever the go-getter agents in his group came looking to make big cases. If we didn't take any chances, Mort seemed to think, then we didn't make any mistakes.

Soon after talking to Berdoo SWAT, I walked into Mort's office and presented my intelligence. "We need to get this guy, Mort," I said. "We need to go up in the hills, grab him by an earlobe, and take his ass right out of his camp. I can get a couple of guys and take him out. But we need to do it soon. He's going to kill someone any day."

Mort stared at me as if he hadn't heard a word I'd just said. "I need your reports caught up before you get into anything else," he said.

I knew he was technically right—at least as far as his admin priorities went. But the way I saw things, Stephens's propensity for violence trumped any backlog of ROIs on my desk. He needed to be taken off the streets before he killed someone.

"I'll catch up on the paper, Mort, but I'm also going to put together a plan to go into the hills and get Stephens."

Mort didn't want to hear it. "Just make sure you get your paper up to speed, Queen."

I left Mort's office discouraged, sat down at my cluttered desk, and scanned the piles of unfinished 3270s.

On one level, I understood where Mort was coming from. To me, he was a classic ATF paper-pusher. His attitude wasn't atypical for a federal law enforcement boss. Group supervisors—special agents in charge (SACs), and assistant special agents in charge (ASACs), whom the rank-and-file agents often call the "adminners"—often have to be persuaded to let the field agents really go out and do their jobs the way the agents want to do them. In my opinion, putting bad guys in jail should always be more important than achieving anyone's personal and political goals. It seemed to me that not everybody acted on this principle. That realization was one of my big disappointments when I became a special agent. Life on the job was a far cry from the image I'd had of my father's rip-roaring career with the feds.

Time and again, it seemed, as in any big bureaucracy, fighting internal battles with my own agency would provide the biggest hurdles in actually putting the bad guys away. We had a saying around the office about the bosses' theory of law enforcement: *Big cases, big problems. Little cases, little problems. No cases, no problems.* The bigger the risks we'd propose in an investigation, the less willing we'd find the administrators to give us the resources to back our play. This philosophy would impact me again and again in my career. Not only was I fighting the bad guys, I often felt like I was fighting recalcitrant federal judges, U.S. attorneys, and my own agency bosses when it came to doing what I was paid to do.

Ask most cops, on a state and local level, and they'll tell you the same stories about the way the criminal justice system functions. But for me, being discouraged from taking risks was a bitter pill to swallow because of the extra intensity and enthusiasm I brought to the job. I got up each morning at three or four, ready to put the bad guys in jail no matter what. Because of my balls-to-the-wall philosophy, I was often at odds with the adminners. Often I didn't hesitate to voice my displeasure—to the detriment of my own career. My reputation within ATF grew as I managed to put together one big case after another, and I was proud to see that I'd become something of a role model to the younger street agents. But I was a never-ending pain in the ass to the administrators.

After my meeting with Jacobson, I called up Special Agent

Wayne Morrison. A seasoned ATF agent assigned to the Arson Group, Wayne was thirty-eight years old and ruggedly good-looking. We'd roomed together in the Inland Empire for a time and had become fast friends.

Wayne was like a rock, one of the most dependable guys on earth—the type of guy who has no problem putting his life on the line for a greater cause. We were a lot alike; he was a former Special Forces and Vietnam vet. In fact, we had chewed some of the same dirt in Vietnam around Da Nang. Wayne and I had similar temperaments and shared the same "street agent" mind-set, a kind of cockiness that led us to believe there was nothing we couldn't do when it came to taking out the bad guys.

"What are you up to, Billy Boy?" Wayne said when he picked up the phone.

"I might have a mission that's right up your alley," I said.

While investigating arsons is an important and rewarding brand of law enforcement, for the most part, it's a paper-chasing proposition and about as exciting as watching ice melt.

"What's the mission?" he asked.

"There's a guy out in our backyard scaring the shit out of all the locals. He's a for-real bad guy. He's a dopehead with an attitude and a machine gun."

"Sounds good," Wayne said.

"There's a catch."

"Yeah?"

"He lives in the Berdoo Mountains."

"How far up?"

"I mean *up* in the mountains. He's been doing this shit for about five years, and no one's been able to catch him. Berdoo SWAT and Fontana SWAT have already given it their best shot. We're going to need to go into the hills and take him right out of his tent."

There was a pause, and then Wayne responded in true Special Forces fashion: "Let me know when you're ready to go get him."

Four

Around the time Mark Stephens crossed my radar, I was
taking on as many cases as my ATF group supervisor
would allow. It's a rare circumstance if you find a detective for a local law enforcement agency, or a special agent for
the federal government, working on just one case at a time; for
the most part, they're juggling several cases.

My group supervisor, Mort Jacobson, seemed to be well
liked by his superior, the special agent in charge of Los Angeles,
Robert Skopeck. At least I thought he was, until certain events
transpired.

I was sitting at my desk typing up 3270s at about seven A.M.
when Skopeck came in. The SAC and I were often the earliest

people in; being first in the office was the way I operated. Sko-peck sauntered over to see what I was up to. Peering over my shoulder, he read as I typed up my report about what I'd been up to the night before.

It had been a routine night of work for an ATF street agent. While working with detectives in Pomona, California, I'd met with two individuals claiming to be members of the Aryan Brotherhood. They'd indicated that they were willing to sell me cocaine and firearms.

In my second report, I typed the name Mark Stephens and identified him as an individual in possession of machine guns.

At approximately nine A.M., Mort Jacobson came in. Sko-peck immediately summoned Mort to his office, and I overheard the RAC (resident agent in charge) and SAC exchange standard salutations. Skopeck questioned Mort about how things were going in the Metro office, and Mort brought him up to speed. I heard Skopeck asking specifically about my work, and Mort briefed him as fully as he could.

I listened as Skopeck's tone changed abruptly. "Did you know that Agent Queen was working undercover and met with members of the Aryan Brotherhood? Did you know that he was setting up drug and gun buys with these people? Did you know about some guy named Mark Stephens who's known to possess a machine gun?"

"No, sir." Since Mort had just made it into the office, he hadn't been briefed by me.

Skopeck suddenly turned loud and belligerent. "Well, why the hell not?" he yelled. "If I know about it, why don't *you*?"

It went on like that for five minutes, Skopeck climbing Mort's ass for knowing less about his own office than the SAC knew. Mort left that meeting looking shaken. I knew he had to be feeling humiliated, and pissed at me for talking with Skopeck before briefing him on my night's activities. He stormed right to my desk in the back of the Metro office.

"What the hell are you doing talking to the SAC and telling him shit before you talk to me?" Mort yelled. "I just got my fuckin' ass chewed because of you, Queen!"

"I didn't tell Skopeck anything," I said. "Hell, he came in the office and read my ROI as I was typing it up."

"Better never let that shit happen again," Mort said, turning and stomping back down the hall to his office. Oh yeah, I thought. I'm going to tell the SAC to buzz off. Right.

I was overcome with frustration. Because of a stroke of bad timing, I had inadvertently pissed off a supervisor who probably wouldn't even let me go near Mark Stephens at this point.

The paperwork was always hard for me. It wasn't that I couldn't do it, but it was like getting a root canal. I would ten times rather be in the streets duking it out with bad guys than sitting at my desk trudging through the paper. And it wasn't only my paperwork that slowed the progress of putting bad guys in jail: Often adminners would load us up with other cases. Later that day, Mort Jacobson walked over to my desk and threw down a relief-of-disability case for me to handle. A relief-of-disability request is an application from a convicted felon to have his rights to possess firearms restored. I had nothing against the program. However, I didn't think it was something a special agent needed to be doing.

But what I thought didn't make any difference; paperwork was part of the job. This particular investigation took me to Claremont, California. While running down information on the relief applicant, I asked a detective in the Claremont Police Department who their most significant troublemaker was. Without hesitation, the detective said, "Mark Stephens." That afternoon I heard more stories about Stephens using violence and intimidation in and around Claremont.

When I got back, I stormed right into Mort's office. I figured even the most unenthusiastic administrator would see the urgency for action on the Stephens case. It all kept running through my head. The assaults, the threats, the automatic weaponry, the criminal violations kept stacking up. Stephens was getting more and more out of control.

"Mort," I said. "I just came back from the Claremont PD and the San Bernardino Sheriff's Department. They all say that somebody has to make another run at catching Stephens."

"Oh yeah?"

"Yeah, and I've been running around for weeks now, trying to do it your way. Stephens keeps terrorizing the Inland Empire, and it seems to me like nobody gives a shit. Nobody's gonna give a shit until he kills someone. So I want to go on record with that."

"Go on record?" Mort had barely bothered to look up from his desk work.

"I've already told everyone here that Stephens is going to

kill. Soon. Mort, how are you going to feel if that happens? When I warned you about it?"

"It's not my call, Queen," he said. "Skopeck's calling the shots on this, not me."

"Then go in there and tell him that Queen said he's going up in the hills to get Stephens before he kills someone. Tell him that, Mort. See what he says."

Mort told me to forget about Stephens and get caught up on my paperwork.

"Jesus Christ," I muttered. When I got back to my desk, I called Wayne Morrison and brought him up to speed on my ongoing battle with the adminners over Mark Stephens. "Christ, Wayne. I'm at wit's end here with the adminners' bullshit. You know what I think we should do?"

"What?"

"I think we ought to go up in the hills and take Stephens out. Just you and me. Fuck the adminners. He's going to kill someone soon, I know it. If we don't take him out, then who the hell is? I can't sit around and wait for this motherfucker to kill. I just can't."

Wayne was a man of few words. "I know, Bill," he said finally. "Just let me know when you're ready to go up there."

"Okay, my man," I said. "Let's talk about it tonight."

It was torturous sitting around the office trying to figure out ways of getting around the RAC and SAC. I knew as I sat there that Stephens was making plans to come down from the hills and hit the community again. I had to convince others in the office that this would happen.

I looked around and saw Jim Cania and Ken Cates planning their next undercover deal. God, I admired those cowboys, especially Cates. They made a great team, and they weren't afraid to mix it up on the baddest side of town. They were always asking me to back their plays.

Ken Cates had come on the job a few weeks before me. He had one blue eye and one brown eye and was a really good-looking guy who drove the girls wild. But he was no lightweight pretty boy. A Vietnam vet from Texas, Cates was a damned good agent who worked tirelessly and had no problem jumping into the deep end. Jim Cania was another hard charger who was constantly ready to mix it up with the bad guys. Cania and Cates were always in the heart of the badlands, where things could go wrong at any time; when you were working South Central, you had to watch your own back while also watching theirs. Two of my own G-ride Mustangs had been shot up while I was backing operations down in South Central. One of them hadn't been on the street for a month before it had bullet holes shot through the front.

I wandered over to Cates's desk. Cania was perched on the corner; they were putting together an ops plan for that evening.

Cania looked at me. "Bill, can you back a UC deal down in gangland tonight?"

"You betcha," I said. I'd much rather be going in after Stephens, but with the adminners' attitude right now, that wasn't going to happen. Working with Cania and Cates would get my mind off the office frustrations.

Backing up your fellow agents always comes first. Even if I

had a stack of unfinished paperwork a foot high on my desk, Mort couldn't say shit about me heading out to work backup on this UC operation. In the back of my mind, I also figured if I kept my stats up, and showed I was a team player by backing Cates and Cania's play, it might give me more leverage to convince Mort that we needed to go after Stephens.

That night's case meant facing off with some violent criminals. Even if it wasn't my operation, it would still be an adrenaline rush. I figured it would give me a different experience and maybe some ideas about how to tackle the Mark Stephens investigation. Cates and Cania undercover were amazing to watch: two white surfer boys hanging out with hard-core South Central L.A. gangsters, buying dope and guns as if they were part of the neighborhood.

It would be Cania and Cates running the op. Howard Sanders, Tom Chumley, and I would back their play. Mort Jacobson would be the supervisor on-scene. It would be a high-risk operation just because of the location in South Central L.A. Extra guns would most definitely be in order.

At approximately seven P.M. we loaded up and met in the parking lot of an abandoned store around Seventy-seventh and Hoover. But then we hit a speed bump. While putting the plan together, Cates had gotten a call from one of his informants, a guy named Nick. Nick was a consistent and reliable CI. He had the gangbanger look and drove an old white van. He wanted to be a cop bad, but being an informant was as close to the action as he could get. Nick loved working for the cops, especially the feds.

By chance, Nick had heard about the location of an ATF fugitive in Watts. We found ourselves between a rock and a hard place. The UC operation was going full speed and couldn't be called off. But the fugitive Nick had located was a dangerous asshole and a top priority for ATF. ATF is constantly targeting gangbangers from the Bloods and the Crips, and any suspect targeted in one of the agency's anti-gang campaigns immediately becomes a priority arrest. In this case, the fugitive was a violent felon wanted on multiple gun and narcotics charges.

Although it was going to make Cates and Cania's op more dangerous, Mort gave me the order. "Okay, Bill," he said. "Take Chumley here and hook up with this Nick. Go grab our fugitive."

Tom Chumley had been in my class at the fed academy, and we'd come on the job together. About thirty-four years old, he was somewhat less athletic than most of us, slightly overweight, and wore glasses. In spite of his appearance, he was not to be underestimated. I had been in several tight places and knew that Chumley was not the type to run.

I called up Nick and set the meet location in Watts. No backup, down in the middle of gangland, ripe with its infamous Crips and Bloods, too little information, and a serious armed bad guy. It was going to be risky business. I loved it.

Chumley and I loaded up and headed out. The streets were already dark. We met Nick at his house and put together an improvised operational plan. Chumley and I would ride down to the meet with Nick in his van. Nick would go inside the fugitive's place and tell him there were a couple of guys outside who wanted to buy some crack. The bad guy would come out with the drugs, and we'd jump him.

.I looked at Chumley. "Ready, buddy?"

"Let's do it."

We headed for the fugitive's place. If I said I wasn't a little nervous, I'd be lying. We rolled into a serious southland gangster-held neighborhood. Nick pulled into the bad guy's driveway, and we all got out of the van. Nick went into the house solo.

I glanced at Chumley. Through my teeth, I whispered, "You know this is one of those shoot-first-ask-questions-later ops, don'tcha?"

Nick came out of the house followed by the bad guy, who looked like a typical gangster: arms prison-yard buff and tattooed up, slouching blue chinos ironed with a razor-sharp crease. He walked up to us with his right hand in his pocket.

I reached out to shake hands with him. "Hey, I'm Bill."

The bad guy didn't take his hand out of his pocket. He shook my right hand with his left. It was obvious he was holding a gun with his other hand. He turned to Chumley and again shook with his left hand. Chumley and I exchanged a look: We knew we were in a bad situation. I started to negotiate with the bad guy over the crack. I told him I wanted to buy an eight ball. We could see from his posture that he was as suspicious of us as we were of him.

Suddenly, it all went south. The bad guy stopped talking. He started to back away from us.

I had to make a move. "He's gonna run!" I yelled at Chumley. I pulled out my gun. "Police!" I screamed. "Motherfucker, don't take another step."

Chumley had his pistol out, too, and he'd cut off the guy's escape route.

I had the barrel of my gun pointed directly at his face. "Here's what you're gonna do, okay?" I said very calmly. "Take your hand out of your pocket slowly, okay? And if anything comes out other than your hand, I'm gonna shoot your fucking face off."

To my dismay, I heard Nick chiming in behind me. "Yeah, motherfucker! I'll blow your black ass up, too."

When I glanced behind me, I saw that Nick had a gun of his own leveled at the fugitive. His expression was crazed, and I bet the bad guy was more worried about Nick than me and Chumley. He slowly started to pull out his hand. I tucked my gun away in my waistband and went for my cuffs. I searched him and found a box cutter in his right pocket. I looked him in the face and said, "So you brought a knife to a gun fight, huh?"

Crisis averted, Chumley and I started breathing normally again. We loaded up the bad guy and headed to jail.

Meanwhile, over in South Central, Cania and Cates had been successful with their undercover op. Nobody got hurt. It had been a good night, a clean sweep for the Metro Group.

The following morning, still in the glow of last night's success, I assumed my stock would be high. It would probably be a good time to hit Mort Jacobson with another request for my mountain-man operation. I was in his office before seven. He would have to be in a good mood after the previous night. We bullshitted for a few minutes about nabbing our fugitive in Watts. Then I started to mention how there was another badass fugitive on ATF's radar screen.

"Listen, Mort, I know you don't really want to hear it, but taking Stephens out—"

Mort cut me off. "Queen, you got your paperwork caught up on from last night?"

"Come on, Mort. The paper ain't shit compared to the Stephens problem. I'm telling you, he's gonna kill someone. You hearing me? He's gonna kill."

"Queen," he said with some exasperation. "Get it through your head. You're not going up in the mountains after that guy. Skopeck's made his decision. He says you can arrest Stephens when he's down from the hills. But you are *not*—you hear me?—going up into the national forest."

It was classic cover-your-ass thinking from the bosses. I had the go-ahead to arrest Stephens when the risks were minimized, when he was down from his mountain hideaway. But how the hell could we predict when that would happen? I knew that in practice, the only way we were going to get him was to go up into the badlands and take him down.

"I can't believe this shit," I said, and I left Mort's office.

Five

Most people don't know that ATF is the premier federal agency charged with enforcing explosives laws in the United States. ATF is the post-blast investigative arm for American law enforcement, which is one reason that ATF and the LAPD's Anti-Terrorist Division work so well together. Over the years, I had made some good friends at the Anti-Terrorist Division.

LAPD detective Al Taylor and I had worked together in the past, taking on neo-Nazis as well as the Crips and the Bloods in Los Angeles. Al's boss, Mike Hillman, was a natural-born leader and a hell of a good cop.

It was about midday when I got the call from Al Taylor. He

said that an LAPD unit had taken a disturbance call in a trailer park down in the San Pedro area and that his office had intel indicating possible terrorist implications. Al told me guns and explosives were involved and that ATF was invited to be part of the investigation.

I shut down my ROI paperwork and headed straight for the door, announcing to Mort Jacobson that I was assisting the LAPD Anti-Terrorist Division on a gun deal. I knew Mort didn't want me doing anything but paper, but I timed my exit perfectly: He was on the phone and couldn't respond quickly enough to stop me. I headed for Parker Center, which was practically right next to the Federal Building on Los Angeles Street. As I walked, I told myself that as long as I kept making good cases, eventually I'd wear Mort down and he'd have no choice but to give me the green light on my mountain-man operation.

I met with Al Taylor downstairs in the lobby. We hit the doors running to the garage and grabbed Al's G-ride. On the way down to San Pedro, Al began bringing me up to speed on the trailer park disturbance call. He said that the complainant had said he'd been threatened by a Middle Eastern guy who had chased him around the neighborhood with a gun, claiming he had machine guns and bombs.

The trailer park was in a heavy-industrial area of San Pedro next to a large oil refinery. Not exactly the high-rent district of the City of Angels. When we arrived at the trailer park, there were several LAPD black-and-whites on the scene, securing the area. Bomb Squad units were on their way, and police had formed a ring around the suspect's residence, bullhorns deployed.

"Everyone inside the trailer! This is the Los Angeles Police Department! Come out with your hands in the air!"

The suspect's wife, a young Middle Eastern–looking woman, came out of the trailer with a child. Then the suspect came out. The LAPD guys were true professionals, and everything went by the book. After the outside parameter was secured, Al and I approached the suspect.

"What's your name?" I said.

After a long staredown, he gave me his name, Muhammad.*

"Well, Muhammad," I said, "I hear that you have machine guns and explosives in your place. Is that true?"

Muhammad stood there with his lips clamped shut. I asked him again, and he stayed silent. Over the years, I'd developed a sense about these moments: I could tell that Muhammad was going to lawyer up if we kept pressing.

Al and I got together with the incident commander and assessed the situation. We felt that we had exigent circumstance with the possibility of explosives in the trailer. We opted for Bomb Squad guys to clear the trailer before anything else. Muhammad, his wife, and their child were removed while the Bomb Squad made their way to the scene. Muhammad's wife was considerably more cooperative than he was. She told us that the suspect was an Iraqi national and that he did have guns and some type of bomb in the trailer.

We learned that Muhammad had left Iraq a few years back to come to America. I talked with the complainant, who told me

---

* Not his real name.

that he had spoken with Muhammad on numerous occasions. He said he had been in Muhammad's trailer before and that Muhammad had shown him guns, including one firearm that he had modified to an easily concealed machine gun by converting the gun to firing fully automatic and sawing off the barrel and stock. The complainant didn't think Muhammad had a job, and he'd seen other Middle Eastern people conversing in Arabic sometimes outside Muhammad's trailer. The complainant was never invited over when Muhammad's acquaintances were there.

After a few minutes, one of the bomb guys came out of the trailer carrying two improvised explosive devices (IEDs) and a couple of firearms. The LAPD secured the trailer, along with Muhammad and his family, while I returned to the office to draw up a federal search warrant.

Obtaining a search warrant in Los Angeles is no walk in the park. There's a specific complaints section at the U.S. Attorney's Office that all the federal agencies use. Before obtaining a warrant, you must first write a detailed affidavit. For an individual who despises paperwork as much as I do, this was always a chore. You then take your affidavit to the complaints section, get in line, and wait for an open assistant United States attorney (AUSA) to review the affidavit.

If the AUSA finds the affidavit sufficient in structure and probable cause, he (or) she will sign off on it and have his secretary fill out the warrant cover sheet and other documents. You present your affidavit to the judge or magistrate along with the warrant documents. After he reviews the affidavit, if he finds sufficient evidence for the warrant to be issued, you will then swear before him that the evidence in the affidavit is the truth to the best of your knowledge.

The judge then signs the warrant and it is registered in the clerk's office, and then you are off to serve it. You have to factor in the intangibles, such as an hour-long wait time because an agent from another department is urgently drawing up a search warrant for Donkey Kong copyright violations.

I returned to San Pedro, warrant in hand, and the search was conducted thereafter. A number of fascinating pieces of evidence besides guns and bombs were discovered during the search of Muhammad's trailer. It seemed that Muhammad had been conducting business with the USSR consulate in San Francisco, a fact proved by documentation we found. More interesting was a stack of money found wrapped in tinfoil: $25,000, to be exact. Wrapped in the money was a note written in Arabic. When we had it translated, it read:

> Dear Lt. Muhammad, here is the money to complete the mission. Please see that these people get paid.

There followed a list of Arabic names.

When I first read the translation, I realized we had likely intercepted a Muslim terrorist about to complete his mission. Muhammad and his accomplices were fixing to blow the hell out of something or somebody. And why was Muhammad so busy visiting with the Soviet consulate in San Francisco? We needed to find out what was up, and fast.

I took another shot at interviewing Muhammad. He was defiant, maintaining a surly disposition, behaving like he was still a soldier for Iraq. Although he had not grown up in the United States, he'd certainly educated himself on his bad-guy rights. We got a pretty clear sense of the guy: He had bullied the community where he lived, but he found out quick that the bully shit didn't work with the police. He glared at us and, at one point, even began screaming angrily and waving his arms. I gritted my teeth and got in his face, eye-to-eye, and told him in no uncertain terms that his ass was mine, that he was going to prison—the only thing in question was for how long. After that, Muhammad turned quiet. An angry, stubborn quiet.

I kept peppering him with questions. "What kind of an asshole keeps bombs in his house with a child and his wife there?" I shouted, getting right in his face. "What if they blew up, asshole? What if you burned your wife and kid alive?"

He remained silent, glaring. I told him I would do my best to send him to prison for as long as I could.

Then Muhammad lawyered up, and we weren't allowed to interview him any longer. ATF and the LAPD's ATD were sufficiently concerned about the threat that we agreed to bring in the FBI. For us, bringing in the FBI was often a last resort; I wasn't happy to be ordered to call the FBI office in downtown San Francisco and coordinate this investigation with them.

My initial contact with the San Francisco FBI office was by

telephone. I identified myself and said that I needed to talk with a special agent about a possible Middle Eastern terrorist plot. The secretary put me on hold. In a few seconds a man answered the phone, identifying himself as an FBI agent, and I told him everything we'd found.

The agent was curt. "So what do you want from us?"

"I want to come up to San Francisco, bring my evidence, and sit down with your office to coordinate this investigation. We believe that the mission these guys were putting together had something to do with San Francisco and the Russian consulate."

"If I were you," the FBI man said, "I wouldn't come up here." He hung up the phone. I was stunned. The correct thing for me to do would have been to notify my office of the FBI's response, but I was so pissed that I got right back on the phone to the FBI. The secretary answered. After a minute or so on hold, the same agent got on the line. I told him I wanted to speak with the group supervisor in the office, and he advised me that was just who he was. I expressed my feelings about how negligently and unprofessionally he had treated me.

Only because he knew he was wrong, he reluctantly agreed to coordinate the investigation with his office; I could come there, and he would hook me up with an agent who worked the Middle East desk. Following the call, I went to my bosses and advised them of how disinterested and unprofessional the FBI was being concerning this investigation. Nonetheless, I made copies of my case files to share with the FBI the following day and made arrangements for Al Taylor and me to travel to San

Francisco. We hopped a plane the following morning, rented a car, and drove to the FBI office.

When Taylor and I arrived, the group supervisor appeared. He didn't invite us into his office but told us to have a seat in the waiting area and he would send someone to talk with us. Taylor and I had sat in the reception area for approximately an hour when I turned to him.

"I've had enough of the bullshit," I said. "You can stay if you want, but I'm out of here."

I packed up my files, and Taylor and I walked out of the office, drove back to the airport, and flew back to L.A. Not a word was said about coordinating investigations with the FBI out of my office following that fiasco.

The general public might have a hard time understanding why two of the premier federal law enforcement agencies, ATF and the FBI—supposedly on the same side in the war against domestic crime and internationally sponsored terror—work so poorly together. I can only relay my own experiences with the FBI. Local cops I worked with almost always spoke about the FBI with utter derision. They felt FBI agents were arrogant, overbearing, and often unprofessional. This was an across-the-board assessment in law enforcement. Very few agencies ever wanted to bring in the FBI on a case.

The FBI's response to my request for assistance was a case in point. I had never had an ax to grind or a bone to pick with them; throughout my career, I simply avoided them as often as I could because of their reputation. My contacts with them were more than 90 percent negative. But I knew one thing for certain:

After the Muhammad arrest, I resolved that I would never ask the FBI for assistance in one of my important investigations. I would never bring them on board in my attempt to apprehend Mark Stephens. I would have to tackle that case using just the resources of ATF and whatever local agencies we could recruit.

Not a word was heard from the FBI about Muhammad until the first Gulf War broke out in 1990. After Operation Desert Storm, the FBI was all over ATF for information on this Iraqi national we had contacted them about four years earlier.

Muhammad was prosecuted for the firearms and improvised explosive devices and went to federal prison.

He never talked about his mission. He never gave up his co-conspirators, and we were never able to uncover their plot. He later applied for U.S. citizenship, and remarkably, although he was a convicted felon who was likely conspiring against the United States, his application for citizenship was granted.

He later sued me and the ATF for slander.

He lost.

Six

It was now just over a month since I'd decided to pick up the lead role in the Mark Stephens investigation. In the midst of getting the runaround from the FBI on the Muhammad case, I got an enormous break in the Stephens investigation: We learned that two of Stephens's former running buddies, Jimmy and Kevin, were willing to meet with me.

By May 1986 all the law enforcement agencies in the Inland Empire were up to speed on the severity of the Stephens problem. The Upland, Fontana, Montclair, Claremont, and Pomona police departments, as well as the San Bernardino sheriff's office, all wanted Stephens. And they knew that a young, hard-charging ATF agent named Billy Queen wanted Stephens, too.

Early one May morning, I got a call from the Claremont detectives saying that they knew of a guy around their community who might have an "in" to Stephens. I shot down to Claremont to hook up with the detectives in hopes of catching a break. They told me about a guy named Kevin who ran a welding shop in Ontario and was known to have sold marijuana for Stephens. They said Kevin wasn't too much of a threat himself; he was a small-time hood and dope dealer. He was also known as a big-time bully in the bars and nightclubs in the area. But detectives had a strong drug case on Kevin and thought he might turn on Stephens, not necessarily because of his drug charges, but because Stephens was threatening him.

To date, he'd shot down all their efforts. But the detectives thought that the sight of a federal agent in Kevin's welding shop might push him over the edge, shock him into cooperating in the search for Stephens.

I strolled into Kevin's welding shop and was surprised by what I saw. Kevin was a damn good welder. An expert, in fact. He'd welded the so-called black boxes used in the airline industry, and I knew that black boxes were made of titanium, which is a difficult metal to work with. I'm not sure how Kevin ended up in business with Stephens, or how a potentially lucrative welding business ultimately led to part-time marijuana dealing and welding up machine guns and hand grenades for a criminal.

Kevin was about six-two and 220 pounds, with calloused hands and a ruddy complexion. He was one of those guys who didn't need much provocation; he just loved to fight. And he told me that he never let it last over a few seconds. Once Kevin's big right hand came down, the fight was usually over. He had the muscles and scars to back his bad-guy reputation.

My first impression was that Kevin was a bit rough around the edges, a tough guy, but not in the mold of a psychopath like Stephens. Kevin was certainly no killer. They say there's no honor among thieves. Throw a healthy dose of fear into the equation and you understand why low-level criminal players like Kevin often roll on their felonious friends.

I identified myself to Kevin as a special agent with the Bureau of Alcohol, Tobacco and Firearms. But I soon saw that Kevin had a more compelling reason for cooperating than the prospect of facing federal gun and explosives charges. Like a lot of other people who'd made the mistake of going into business with Stephens, Kevin initially hadn't been clear on how violent and dangerous an individual Stephens could be. It wasn't long before he got a firsthand glimpse of Stephens's true nature.

As big and bad as Kevin was, he was scared to death of his former friend. By the time I interviewed him, Kevin was wishing he had never laid eyes on Mark Stephens. The business of simply selling marijuana for Stephens had seemed like a good idea at the time, he said, but quickly had turned into a nightmare. Kevin didn't have a problem with beating up someone who'd pissed him off, but he wasn't up for a murder. He wouldn't have dreamed of committing the violence Stephens was all too eager to dole out to anyone who got on his bad side—including Kevin.

For weeks Kevin had been ducking and dodging Stephens because he was unable to pay Stephens some dope money he owed him. He'd come to work in his shop one day, figuring he'd put in eight hours of welding, hit a few bars, and then head home. It was hotter than normal in the Inland Empire, and Kevin had opened all the shop doors and cranked the fans. If he had that day to live over again, he told me, he would have kept the doors closed and sweated it out locked in the shop.

Around two in the afternoon, Stephens walked into the shop. He startled Kevin in the middle of a welding job. Stephens loomed over Kevin with his MAC-10 in hand. Kevin dropped his welding torch and stood up to face Stephens, trying to make light of the fact that Stephens was armed, but Stephens wasn't in a joking mood.

He demanded to know where the thousand dollars was that Kevin owed him for grass sold on consignment. Kevin tried to stall, telling Stephens he needed a few more days to get the money together.

Stephens wasn't interested in hearing it. When Kevin turned away from Stephens, he caught a glimpse in his peripheral vision of the machine gun following his head. Stephens shoved the barrel right up against Kevin's skull. Kevin froze, feeling the cold barrel tickle his ear. Stephens snatched Kevin by the collar and shoved him down with the MAC-10 secured against his head.

Then Stephens squeezed the trigger. Only at the last moment did he jerk the MAC-10 barrel a few inches up. There was a deafening fire burst as Stephens proceeded to blast twenty rounds inside the shop, blowing holes in the walls and windows. Kevin clutched at his near-deafened ears, falling to his knees, and watched as Stephens quickly popped another clip in the machine gun. On his knees in prayer, stunned and shaking, Kevin kept promising over and over that he'd do whatever Stephens wanted.

"Next time I see you," Stephens said, "you fuckin' better have my money."

As hard a character as Kevin was, his running buddy Jimmy was ten times harder. The intel I gathered from the various local police and sheriff's departments indicated that Jimmy was one of the Inland Empire's most feared bad guys. Jimmy seemed to be up to his butt in cops all the time—he had a rap sheet a yard long. He wasn't as physically imposing as Kevin or Mark Stephens, but he more than made up for his size with badass attitude. He'd spent much of his adult life behind bars and had that instantly recognizable, heavily tattooed, prison-hardened physique and mind-set. I think that was why Jimmy figured he could dance with the devil, that he and Mark Stephens would make a good criminal partnership. And so Jimmy had agreed to sell grass for Stephens around the Inland Empire and to do whatever else Stephens asked. At first they got along. Jimmy knew all about Stephens's hot-headed propensity for violence, but it was a gamble he figured was worth taking.

From time to time, Jimmy told me, Stephens would get lonely in the mountains. Although Stephens had the animals to talk to, they couldn't substitute for human contact. And so Stephens invited Jimmy to live and work with him at his mountain retreat. One day Stephens and Jimmy made their way on foot from the valley to their mountain hideaway. They crossed nice suburban streets and yards. When Jimmy and Stephens reached the fence to one family's backyard, Stephens suddenly stopped. He stood and watched a young father playing with his son in the yard.

Jimmy said nothing, just watched Stephens glaring at the father and son. There was intense hatred in Stephens's stare, Jimmy later told me. Then Stephens began to clench his jaw and grimace. Jimmy looked back at the father and son playing ball.

Finally, Stephens began to speak. "Just look at that shit," he said. "I never had fun with my father like that." Stephens's face turned bright red. "Fuckin' pisses me off. How come I never played with my father like that?"

Jimmy stood back a few steps as Stephens began to work himself into a fury.

"I ought to fuckin' kill them," Stephens said.

"What for?" Jimmy said.

"I never had fun like that." Stephens kept glaring at the unsuspecting father and son, his face darkening by the second. "Yeah . . . I ought to fuckin' kill them."

Jimmy watched as Stephens put his hand on his gun. He gritted his teeth and began to shake with tremors. "Yessir, I'm gonna kill them . . . I'm gonna fuckin' kill them."

Stephens had worked himself into a trance. Jimmy began to try to reason with him, but it seemed too late. Stephens didn't hear a word he was saying.

"Mark, man, snap out of it," Jimmy said, "they haven't done anything to you. You don't want to hurt them, they haven't done anything."

By now Stephens had a tight grip on his gun and was checking the magazine. "I'm gonna kill them," he kept muttering. "I'm gonna kill them."

Jimmy knew he had to stop him; he couldn't let Stephens shoot the two unsuspecting people.

"Mark!" he yelled at the top of his voice. He grabbed Stephens's muscular forearm. "Mark! Look at me, man! Let's go! These fuckin' people haven't done anything."

The shouting seemed to break Stephens's trance. He looked at Jimmy as if he'd just come to from a long, fitful sleep.

"Let's get out of here," Jimmy said.

"Yeah, okay," Stephens answered. "Let's go."

Jimmy never felt fully safe around Mark Stephens after that day.

For weeks Jimmy continued to work with Stephens up in the mountains. He helped carry water to the marijuana plants. He dug up weeds and did chores around the camp. At night they would sit around a campfire and talk about how rich they were going to be one day. Stephens told Jimmy how he was putting together an arsenal of hand grenades and one day soon would start blowing the hell out of people. People who pissed him off. People like that fucking father and son playing in their backyard with their stupid smiling faces. The more Mark Stephens talked, the more Jimmy realized his newfound friend was drifting back and forth between reason and insanity.

Every so often, much to Jimmy's dismay, Stephens would go into a murderous trancelike state like the one Jimmy had witnessed with the father and son. Jimmy could no longer reason with Stephens. And the longer Jimmy stayed up in the San Bernardino Mountains, the more his presence seemed to trigger Stephens's irrational mood swings. He would become enraged for no apparent reason. Jimmy was a convenient target: Stephens needed to vent, and Jimmy was the only one around. Stephens began to look harder and harder at Jimmy during his tirades about hurting people. He would strap on his MAC-10 submachine gun while menacingly grinning at Jimmy.

The hardened lifelong criminal in Jimmy knew what was what, that it was only a matter of time before Stephens went into one of his trances and killed him in a flash of 9mm bullets.

Jimmy made up his mind. He had to get out of Stephens's camp soon or he'd never be seen again. His bones would be picked clean by coyotes and scavengers. But he also knew that if he abandoned Stephens, it would be just the excuse the man needed to come track him down. It was a no-win situation for Jimmy, but he opted for flight and picked a time to escape.

It was the dead of night. Jimmy lay in his tent staring up at the stars, waiting for the sound of his companion's snoring.

When he was sure Stephens was asleep, he'd make a break for it. He knew that if Stephens caught him slipping out of the camp, he'd get his brains blown out. But he didn't have any choice. Jimmy was sure Stephens was going to kill him anyway.

In the early-morning darkness, Jimmy climbed out of his tent. He stumbled through the darkness toward the trail that led down the mountain. If he made the least little noise, it would alert Stephens, and he would die. He crept along by inches, terrified that Stephens would jump up and catch him.

Hours passed as Jimmy crept blindly along the mountain path. He wasn't sure Stephens hadn't woken up, flanked him, and waited for him behind the next bush or tree. Only a few more feet, he told himself over and over. He kept telling himself that until the darkness turned to first light.

In the dawn, Jimmy began to run until at last he was at the bottom of the mountain. He had made it down, but he was hardly home free. Jimmy would have to keep running from Stephens for as long as he lived anywhere near Los Angeles.

In early May 1986, a month and a half into the Stephens investigation, I convinced Kevin to set up a meet for me with Jimmy. After that brief foray into the mountains, Jimmy was convinced that somebody was going to die soon, and he damn sure didn't want to be the victim.

The meet was set for a Denny's in Ontario, and though I knew Jimmy was a hard-core criminal with prison time, I didn't bring backup; I didn't think Kevin would be foolish enough to try setting me up for a bad meet. I showed up for the meet alone and took my place in a quiet booth near the back. Kevin soon joined me. At around seven P.M. Jimmy walked up to our booth.

Jimmy had dark hair and stood about five feet seven, at 150 pounds. I knew he'd done his time in a variety of California state prisons. He was quick to augment his hand-fighting skills with knives, hammers, wrenches, or whatever else was within reach. He wasn't the kind of guy you could easily intimidate, but I knew he wanted to talk to me.

Jimmy sat down next to Kevin and didn't say a word to me. Kevin did the introductions.

Jimmy reached across the booth to shake. He had a rough, calloused palm and a wiry forearm covered in blue prison ink.

"Good to meet you, Jimmy," I said.

"Good to meet you."

I let Kevin take the lead in the conversation. He looked at me and said, "Stephens is fucking nuts, Queen, I'm telling you."

Jimmy chimed in, "Yeah, Queen. You got your work cut out for you. You better be damn careful fooling around with this fuckin' guy."

Jimmy said that Stephens was an unpredictable guy to begin with, but add some drugs to him and he was a truckload of trouble. Stephens could handle more drugs than anyone Jimmy had ever seen. Once Stephens had dropped close to twenty tabs of acid. He was lucky he hadn't permanently fried his brain.

Jimmy told me about heading up to the hills with Stephens. He said he knew that if he hadn't left when he did, Stephens would have killed him within days. He had seen Stephens go into tirades that not only scared the shit out of his victims, they scared the shit out of Jimmy, too.

Kevin chimed in, saying it was only a matter of weeks before Stephens killed someone.

I asked them for details about Stephens's firepower. They both said that he would have me outgunned at any time. They had both seen Stephens in possession of handguns, machine guns, and hand grenades, and they had both seen his expertise in using them.

Jimmy went on to tell me, as best as he could recall, how to get to Stephens's camp off El Cajon Pass. But knowing the general coordinates was barely half the battle. Jimmy had never been anywhere more remote and desolate than that camp. He said I could probably follow Stephens's trail, but I needed to beware of booby traps, and he couldn't recall precisely where Stephens had set them. And the camp was at the top of an area where he could survey everyone coming for miles.

The waitress brought over our check. Before we got up, I nodded at Jimmy. "If Stephens does spot me coming up the trail after him, what am I in for? What can I expect?"

Jimmy looked me dead in the eye, shrugged, and used a phrase that would echo in my head repeatedly in the weeks and months to come.

"Queen, if he spots you coming up that trail—he's gonna blow you outta your fuckin' socks."

Seven

Every day I was gathering more intel on Stephens, driving around the Inland Empire in my Mustang convertible, and outlining a prospective takedown in my mind. But I still didn't have the green light to put together an ops plan. My supervisors at Metro Group were nowhere near ready to give me the go-ahead for such a high-risk operation. Time and again they argued that there would be hell to pay within the Bureau if I jeopardized my life or the lives of other ATF agents by attempting to go up into the San Bernardino National Forest. Their attitude continued to be: *Let the locals deal with him. Or grab Stephens sometime when he comes down to civilization.*

Even as I continued to strategize on how to get around the

bureaucratic hurdles, I found myself working an undercover buy-and-bust operation that soon spiraled out of control. From time to time I would go into my undercover mode as Billy St. John, a Harley-riding badass dopehead from the South. I was still in the early stages of forming that persona, going UC mostly on short-term operations. I never imagined that the identity would become my full-time law enforcement persona a decade later, in the late nineties, when I found myself infiltrating the outlaw motorcycle gang underworld in a landmark twenty-six-month investigation against the Mongols.

I caught a break in my constant interoffice wrangling at ATF. Mort Jacobson got bounced upstairs, and I had a new group supervisor, a Vietnam vet whose leadership style was much more suited to my own. Mort had been somewhat less than enthusiastic about getting into the trenches with the bad guys; as far as he was concerned, an adopted case was as good as an initiated ATF investigation. But it had been tough for Mort, because he had had more than his share of go-getters to handle: cowboys like Ken Cates and Jim Cania, Lanny Royer and Mike Matassa. Royer and Matassa were the salt of the earth—both damn good investigators and guys you could depend on. We all had an infectious spirit and enthusiasm for the job.

Our new group supervisor was Special Agent Chuck Pratt. Pratt was a former marine and had been assigned to L.A. Metro for only a couple of months. He'd been a field agent in San Francisco and had just been promoted to group supervisor and transferred down to Los Angeles. For me, he was a welcome relief. I didn't want to push him too soon, but I did have some hope that he would see how imperative it was to go into the hills to get Mark Stephens.

Not long after taking the reins, Pratt got a call from a special agent named Steve Fitzpatrick, who was working out of the ATF office in Reno, Nevada. Fitzpatrick had gotten a call from a reliable CI who said that an acquaintance of his wanted to dump a load of C-4. C-4 is a high-velocity explosive that resembles ordinary plastic and has a texture similar to ridged putty. It is manufactured for military use only; if civilians have it in their possession, it's most likely stolen. Fitzpatrick's bad guys claimed to have 250 pounds of the stuff. They also had a bunch of liquid PCP and some guns with silencers they wanted to get rid of. Fitzpatrick relayed the phone number of one of the bad guys to Chuck Pratt.

Pratt was initially skeptical. The deal seemed too good to be true. Guns, silencers, PCP, and a huge quantity of contraband military explosives sounded like a police sting.

I overheard Pratt's end of the conversation. "Steve," he said, "I've got an agent here I want you to talk to. If it is for real, he can put it together. He's another old Vietnam vet like us. His name is Bill Queen."

I picked up the phone and heard the same story that Fitzpatrick had told Pratt. And I had the same gut feeling.

"It's either a police sting," I told Fitzpatrick, "or a pile of horseshit. Nobody sells explosives, guns, silencers, and dope together in one neat little package. That kind of shit only happens in the movies. But hell, you never know. Lemme put in a cold call to the bad guys."

When you're working undercover, it's always most desirable to have a confidential informant make a face-to-face introduction to your intended target. But sometimes you have no choice but to make cold calls to the bad guys. I told Fitzpatrick to call his CI back and tell him to inform the bad guys in L.A. that a dopehead by the name of Billy St. John would be giving them a call.

I waited a day or so before I put in my cold call. Pratt and I talked about the situation, and both of us thought how unlikely it would be for this thing to be a real deal. But we didn't have the luxury of assuming it was bogus: The idea that 250 pounds of high-velocity military explosives would be hitting the streets of L.A.—likely making its way into the hands of warring gang-bangers and other criminal groups—compelled us to follow up immediately.

Fitzpatrick called from Reno to say he'd talked with his CI, who was making the call to L.A. at that very moment. So far, things were going like clockwork—highly unusual when dealing with real-life bad guys. We have a slang term in law enforcement for the pace at which street hoods operate: "drug-dealer time." If the perps say they'll meet you in half an hour, that could mean anywhere between twenty-four minutes and twenty-four hours. Working on drug-dealer time, you just never know.

These guys were punctual, which made it all the more likely in my mind that we were dealing with other cops. Fitzpatrick called back with the green light, saying everything had been set up for my cold call. Fitz gave me the number and told me I should ask for a guy named John. John and his buddies were eager to do the deal, he said.

I walked over to Chuck Pratt's office and told him that if ever there was an investigation out of the Metro Group office that needed to be run through L.A. CLEAR, this was it. L.A. CLEAR is a clearinghouse operation to which law enforcement agencies throughout the area can submit their investigations to see if other agencies are working the same targets. Using the limited information I had, I ran our buy-and-bust through the CLEAR system. Checking at least reassured me that if there were an agency setting up a dope, guns, silencers, and explosives deal in the Los Angeles region, my inquiry would ring some bells.

But overlapping cases prove to be more problematic than just two rival spiderwebs tangling up. If you unwittingly step into another undercover operation, the outcome can be potentially fatal. You can wind up with cops pulling guns on other cops—without either side being certain that the others aren't legitimate bad guys.

Word came back that there was no other law enforcement agency in the L.A. area orchestrating this deal. I contacted ATF intelligence and ran the telephone number I'd been given for the bad guys by Fitzpatrick's CI. No luck. It was a cell phone and unregistered. To track down the name behind an unregistered cell phone would require a subpoena, and there was no way we had time for that courthouse tango.

If this was a real deal, what kind of guys would be holding 250 pounds of stolen C-4? A foreign or homegrown terrorist cell? But terrorists weren't likely to dabble in PCP; nor would they likely be trying to unload a bunch of handguns with silencers. If you're a terrorist, you can never have enough guns or high-grade plastic explosives. Ex–U.S. military guys? Military guys wouldn't be in possession of silencers unless they had a special-ops background. As a former Special Forces soldier, I knew there weren't any special-ops units based in L.A.—the nearest being the Navy SEALs down in San Diego—and I considered it pretty unlikely that SEALs would be dabbling in PCP.

What kind of crew was I tangling with here? High explosives, PCP, and guns with silencers made for a diverse group of bad guys, to say the least. The more I mulled it over, the more I realized I would need some heavy-duty backup from ATF and the LAPD. Steve Fitzpatrick had said that he was jumping on the next plane from Reno, but I would need a lot more for backup.

I put in a call to my friend Al Taylor, from the LAPD's Anti-Terrorist Division, who'd recently worked the Muhammad investigation with me. Like Pratt and Fitzpatrick, Al was a former marine. Luckily, it seemed like I was surrounded by jarheads.

"Al, you want to work some today?"

"What's up, Billy?"

"There's a guy here in L.A. who says he's got a shitload of C-4, some guns with silencers, and a bunch of liquid PCP."

"Sounds like a sting to me," Al said.

"I know, but I ran it through L.A. CLEAR and it came up clean. We got a phone number for the bad guys, and it's an unlisted cell. You never know, Al."

"Right, you never know," Al said. "Then again, it might be a rip."

A "rip"—or rip-off—is a bogus deal set up by criminals to rob other criminals, usually drug dealers. Rips are one of the great risks of undercover work and one of the biggest reasons undercover agents get killed in the line of duty.

"I guess. Maybe it could be a rip," I said. But I didn't really want to think much about that scenario. If anything, I'd make sure I was loaded up to the max on this one. I wanted as much backup as I could possibly have. Al said he could scare up a few guys from his office. "Just keep me up to speed on what's cooking," he said.

I spent the next hour and a half doing the paperwork needed to get the investigation off the ground: a standard 3270 ROI; an electronic surveillance request to tape conversations; a request for agent cashier funds to purchase evidence if our sting operation got that far.

At approximately twelve-thirty P.M., I was ready to put in the first phone call to the bad guys. I had no idea what to expect. I wired the phone in the undercover room for audiotape and put in the call.

A man answered on the second ring. "Hello?"

"Yeah, this is Billy St. John," I said, using a gruff take-no-bullshit tone. "Look, is John there?"

"This is John."

"John, I guess we got a mutual friend in Reno, huh?"

"Yeah, I guess we do."

"Listen, I hear you got some—uh—stuff that I might be interested in."

John stunned me with his response. He didn't bother with even rudimentary criminal code; he gave me an outright inventory of his wares, which the rolling federal-government Nagra beside me captured in crystal-clear Dolby sound.

"I got about two hundred and fifty pounds of C-4," he said. "I also got a few guns and silencers, and I got about a hundred and eighty ounces of liquid PCP. You interested in any of it?"

Jesus Christ, I thought, *if this isn't a cop sting, this perp has got to be in the running for the all-time-top-ten list of the country's dumbest criminals.*

"You never know," I said. "I'm gonna have to take a look at the stuff before I can say anything definite. You understand, right? So listen, when can I see it?"

His answer stunned me again.

"Let's do it today."

The freight train was moving, and I wasn't going to be the one slamming on the brakes.

"Cool. How much you want for the stuff?"

"For which?"

"For all of it."

He began running down the list, rattling off prices. I couldn't believe what I was hearing. It was kind of like being at the checkout line in a bad-guy supermarket.

"Okay, but first things first. Let's meet so I can take a look at the stuff," I said.

"That sounds good," he said. "But loading up all two hundred and fifty pounds of C-4 doesn't make any sense. I'll bring you a taste. How about twenty-five pounds of the C-4, some of the PCP, and some guns with silencers? If that works out, then we'll set up another day when you can buy the rest."

"Sounds like a good deal to me," I said.

John asked me if I knew the Denny's on Ventura Boulevard in Woodland Hills.

"Sure." I didn't have a clue, but I knew I wouldn't have much trouble finding the place.

"Meet me there about five today."

"You're on," I said.

"How'm I gonna know you?"

"Let's see. I'll be wearing a green ball cap."

Things were now going into overdrive. I told Chuck Pratt that I had a deal set up at a Denny's in Woodland Hills to buy the guns, silencers, PCP, and twenty-five pounds of explosives. The paperwork was completed. Backup was notified. The meeting was set. Whether the case was a righteous deal, a rip, or a police sting, there was no turning back now.

I called 411 and got the number and address for Denny's. Then I dialed up Al Taylor and told him we were on for a five P.M. meet with the bad guys up in Woodland Hills.

"Why the hell did you set it for five?" Al said. "This is L.A.—you got any idea what traffic is going to be like at that time?"

"Yo, dude. I didn't set the deal up. These assholes set it up. They made it for a Denny's. It's a public place, not very conducive for a rip. Didn't figure I'd haggle over the time or the traffic situation."

"That's why you're a fed." Al laughed. He had been in the

cop business in L.A. for a long time; he said the traffic situation would have been one of the first things calculated in a buy-and-bust deal.

And it turned out that traffic did become one of the biggest factors in this operation—just not for the obvious reasons.

Back when I was a kid in the hills of North Carolina, we had a saying about fishing: *You catch 'em, you clean 'em.* It was pretty much the same for an ATF undercover operation back in the mid-eighties. It was up to the undercover to make sure he'd covered all the bases in order to cover his own ass. Chuck Pratt was getting the money to buy the evidence, and I was pulling in the tech guys to help with electronic surveillance.

Two bad guys were supposed to make the meet with me. We later learned their criminal pedigrees. John Sergeant and Steve Pajack were small-time crooks trying to up their status in the L.A. area. They may have been experts when it came to selling guns and dope, but with military explosives, as I was to see first-hand, either they were in way over their heads or they possessed a serious death wish.

I knew they were bringing two vehicles to the meet. Obviously, we had to assume that both Sergeant and Pajack would be armed with handguns.

At three P.M. a pre-op brief was held at the L.A. Metro office. Representing the ATF were me, Chuck Pratt, Steve Fitzpatrick, Jerry Petrelli (an ATF agent and former marine out of New York), and Howard Sanders. Sanders and I had come on the job about the same time. We made friends quickly and remained that way. Petrelli was a former marine and Vietnam vet. We also became longtime friends, and we would later serve together on the ATF Special Response Team. He was wounded at the Branch Davidian siege in Waco in 1993. Al Taylor was representing the LAPD. He would later brief the other LAPD officers assigned to take part in the operation. Everyone around the room had their game faces on. There were no illusions for anyone about undercover operations' potential to suddenly turn bad.

Since explosives were involved, Al Taylor notified the LAPD Bomb Squad. The plan was for Fitzpatrick to go with me to Denny's. I would hold the cash and buy the guns, dope, and explosives, along with any other prohibited items the bad guys may bring to the scene. If I found that things were too dangerous or getting out of hand, or if the operation needed to be aborted for any reason, my signal to initiate the takedown would be to take off my green hat.

We each knew what we had to do. We all saddled up and hit the road.

Fitzpatrick and I rolled into Denny's early and found a booth. ATF regulations would have preferred that we order coffee or Coke, but in the real world of bad-guy protocol, a couple of Budweisers seemed more appropriate. We were nursing our beers for a few minutes before two men walked in, one fitting the description John had given me over the phone.

John looked around and walked straight up to me. "You Billy?"

I stood up. We shook hands. "Yeah, I'm Billy. And this is my friend Steve."

John narrowed his eyes. He was skeptical. Then he nodded at his running buddy. "Well, this is *my* friend Steve."

I squinted at him. "Okay, two Steves."

We sat down in the booth. John took the lead by assuring us that everything they had was good shit. They'd held up their end, brought everything they'd said they would be bringing, and could furnish us with all the guns and explosives we needed. And if this deal went well, John said, he could get us hand grenades and any kind of dope we wanted.

"That's great," I said. "But let's get past this deal first."

Bad-guy Steve looked at John. "Take him out to the car and show him the stuff," he said.

"Good deal."

John and I got up and left the two Steves inside Denny's. Once outside, we turned away from the parking area and headed for the street. I didn't say a word. When we reached the sidewalk, John pointed to a parking lot across the street. "I left my car over there."

I was stunned. He'd parked in the lot for Taft High School. This was potentially bad. There were dozens of other cars parked there, and activities were still going on at the school. I could hear kids' voices in the distance, and a few laughing teenagers were filtering out of the back doors into the parking lot.

We walked across Ventura Boulevard to the school parking lot. As we approached John's Ford, I could hardly believe it; ironically, his California license plate ended with the letters ATF.

John went right to the back of the car, stuck the key in the lock, and popped open the trunk to reveal a large red plastic camping cooler. He opened it. Initially, the only thing I could see inside was a green wool army blanket, which John jerked back.

Holy shit. What immediately grabbed my attention were about a dozen electrical blasting caps sitting right on top of the twenty-five pounds of C-4. John was babbling away about the quality of the goods. He gestured to a lab-type bottle containing a large quantity of liquid PCP. I don't think I heard a word he was saying; my eyes were fixed on the blasting-cap wires. They weren't shunted. Unshunted blasting-cap wires are a disaster waiting to happen; sitting on top of twenty-five pounds of high explosives, they had the potential to blow not just the parking lot but the entire high school into the stratosphere.

John snatched up one of the firearms—a SIG-Sauer 9mm—and handed it to me to examine. He was so brazen in his movements. God and everybody in Woodland Hills could see him. Though he was telling me all about the silencer attached to the gun, I still found it impossible to concentrate on anything but the explosives. I handed the gun back to John. He threw it haphazardly back in the cooler, sending the blasting caps flying.

John wanted to go on with his presentation, but I'd seen all I wanted to see inside that cooler.

"Okay," I finally said. "Good enough. Let's head back over to Denny's."

He looked a bit crestfallen, like he wasn't through with the demonstration, but the look of resolve on my face told him we were. My heart stopped beating again when he roughly threw that wool blanket back into the cooler. This knucklehead obviously had no idea what he was dealing with, but I knew full well that just one small crackle of static electricity from the blanket and this entire undercover operation would be front-page headline news in tomorrow's *Los Angeles Times*. John slammed the trunk shut and turned to walk back with me across the street.

As we crossed, I tried to act relaxed, all the while thinking how unbelievably stupid these bad guys were. I was also thinking, *Ain't no way I'm buying this shit right here in the parking lot. Ain't no way I'm letting anyone, other than the LAPD Bomb Squad, try to handle this shit.* Right now the most important thing was getting myself and everyone else in Woodland Hills out of this UC deal alive.

John walked a few steps in front of me, and I could see the outline of a gun in his back pocket. Enough was enough. I was putting an end to this op *now.*

I reached up and took my hat off, knowing that in seconds my guardian angels would be screaming in to take control of the crime scene.

A few seconds passed. Nothing. *My boys probably didn't see me,* I thought. I took my hat off again when we reached the curb. Still nothing. I took my cap off one more time and tossed it the air. Nothing. I could see that Steve Pajack, the other bad guy, had exited Denny's and gone to his pickup truck.

Shit, was I going to have to take these guys down myself? All at once the cache of explosives across the street concerned me less than the outline of the gun in John's back pocket. I made one more attempt at calling in the cavalry. Just as John and I reached Denny's, Pajack pulled up in his truck right beside the entrance door.

At long last I heard the sounds of engines revving and tires squealing as my backup roared in. Unfortunately, John and Pajack also heard the cops rolling in. John immediately upped the ante, going for the gun in his pants.

I went into survival mode. It was too late to try to pull my own pistol. I leaped like a linebacker and tackled John, knocking him up against the front of Pajack's truck. Steve Fitzpatrick immediately reacted, pulling his firearm and jumping up on the truck's running board.

"Freeze!" he shouted, pointing his gun at Pajack. "Freeze, motherfucker!"

John and I were tussling over his pistol. He still hadn't gotten it out of his pants, and I had his forearms locked in a vise grip. If Pajack decided to make a run for it, I realized, he was going to run over both me and his idiot partner in crime.

Al Taylor was the first LAPD backup on the scene, and he used all his strength to hit John.

"He's got a gun!" I yelled.

Al immediately went to work on John's head, pummeling him mercilessly. John let go of his gun, and I wrestled it free. Al and several other LAPD cops pulled John to the ground, muscled his arms back, and cuffed him while Fitzpatrick and Petrelli pulled Pajack from the truck. In seconds both were safely cuffed and under arrest.

Round one was over. Chuck Pratt and everyone else gathered around me, wanting details on why we'd aborted the buy-and-bust operation in midstream.

When I could see that John and Pajack no longer posed a threat, I hit Pratt with the bad news.

"Across the street," I said, "we got a giant PCP bomb waiting to go off."

"A what?"

I told Al Taylor he needed to get the Bomb Squad on the scene pronto. Not only had the bad guys delivered what they'd said they would deliver, they'd thrown about a dozen blasting caps into the mix.

"Blasting caps?" Pratt was incredulous.

"No," I said. "Not just blasting caps. *Electrical* blasting caps. And to make things even more interesting, the electrical blasting caps are sitting right on top of the C-4. Oh, and tell the Bomb Squad the blasting caps are unshunted."

Al Taylor called his bosses at LAPD and then notified the Bomb Squad while Pratt notified the L.A. special agent in charge. A number of LAPD black-and-whites began arriving to assist in securing the scene.

Within thirty minutes, the first Bomb Squad team was on the scene. One of the first guys to arrive was a friend of mine named Dave Weller. I told Dave what kind of party was waiting for him in the cooler across the street. Dave's face completely drained of color. More Bomb Squad guys kept arriving, and then the brass started to show up.

That's when the shit hit the fan. The first thing the brass wanted to know was why an ATF agent had set up a high-explosive and PCP deal in a goddamned high school parking lot. Dozens more cops were rolling in from all directions. The order was given to evacuate Taft High School.

Denny's was located just off the 101, one of the most heavily trafficked freeways in America. Within minutes, the 101 was completely shut down in both directions.

Right next to Taft High School was the quiet residential neighborhood of Woodland Hills. Cops began to evacuate every house in the neighborhood. *Shit,* I thought, *even if the bomb doesn't blow, this clusterfuck is still going to make the front page of the* L.A. Times.

I'd thought we had everything under control. But the LAPD Bomb Squad had put the image in the minds of the brass that a giant cloud of vaporized PCP could soon be drifting through Woodland Hills, sending thousands of people throughout the San Fernando Valley into neverland. The LAPD brass was pissed that some ATF agent would jeopardize the citizens of L.A. like that.

I couldn't do anything but stand by and watch as the Bomb Squad took over my operation. Dave Weller put on his bomb suit and approached John Sergeant's Ford. I prayed that Weller would secure the explosives without those unshunted blasting caps blowing up. From my background as a Green Beret, I knew that the bomb suit he had on wasn't going to save him if the C-4 detonated. The best it would do was keep his body parts in one location somewhere in Woodland Hills.

The brass kept asking me why I'd set up the undercover deal in a high school parking lot. I kept trying to explain that we'd agreed to meet at Denny's, and I'd had no idea these idiots would be leaving their merchandise in a high school lot, let alone have transported the explosives, drugs, and unshunted blasting caps in one Coleman cooler.

At my wits' end, I suggested we send John Sergeant across the street to remove the blasting caps from the cooler himself. He was too stupid to understand the mortal danger he was in. Maybe his idiot's blind luck would hold up.

Even if this turned out well, I knew I'd probably be in purgatory for the next year, typing up ATF reports and justifying myself to the LAPD and the brass in Washington, D.C. I watched Dave Weller as he began removing items from the cooler. So far, so good.

Chuck Pratt told me to get a couple of guys and head to the slammer with Pajack and Sergeant. Although I wanted to stay until the scene was secured, Pratt was right. We needed to continue securing the perps and start the process of locking them up.

It was an important bust for ATF, in spite of the well-publicized bomb scare. In fact, the manner in which the arrests of John Sergeant and Steve Pajack went haywire only made me more resolved about putting together an airtight ops plan for going after Mark Stephens. I knew it would only be a matter of time before I could convince Chuck Pratt that we needed to get Stephens. And when I did get approval to go after the mountain man, I would make sure not a single detail in the ops plan was left to chance.

Eight

hile I was busy collaring John Sergeant and Steve Pajack in the San Fernando Valley, Mark Stephens was ratcheting up his reign of terror in San Bernardino County. It had been two months since I'd been on the case, and much to my frustration, I was no closer to getting my shot at taking him down. But now it wasn't just Stephens's drug-dealing partners who had to worry about him. No one in the Inland Empire who came into contact with him was safe from his fury, including his own parents.

Mike Vaughn was a friend of mine with the LAPD. Like me, he was a biker chaser, meaning he belonged to a select group of cops from all over the area who were always keeping an eye on the outlaw motorcycle gangs (OMGs). Mike and I would end up working OMGs together later on, first when I was hanging out with the Hells Angels and then when I went undercover inside the Mongols.

By coincidence, Mike Vaughn lived in Rancho Cucamonga, on Valley Street, right across the street from Mark Stephens's parents. Long before Stephens hit my radar, Mike was well aware of his gun-toting tirades.

One day Mike Vaughn had been doing intelligence work, gathering and sharing information with other agencies around L.A. on the motorcycle gangs in the area. Gangs like the Mongols, the Vagos, and Hells Angels were on the rise in the L.A. area, and their penchant for violence kept Mike and law enforcement agents in Southern California busy. Mike was looking forward to coming home to a peaceful, relaxed evening. But when he turned the corner onto Valley Street, he saw that he'd rolled headlong into a domestic disturbance call, like so many he'd responded to in his early days as a cop. The only difference was, this one was playing out right on his own block.

Mike watched as Mark Stephens's mother stood in front of her house, screaming and trying to fight off her attacker. But this wasn't a drunken husband or home invader who was attacking her—it was her own son, whom Mike had encountered a few times in the past. Stephens had busted a spring and gone off over a simple disagreement with his mother, and he had her bundled in his muscle-bound arms and was trying to stuff her through the window of her car. Mike bailed out of his car and ran to help. Stephens knew who Mike was; as deranged and hotheaded as Stephens was, he wasn't about to take on the cops on this day. He threw his mother down on the pavement and bolted for his hideout in the hills.

Stephens's parents, despite their best efforts to raise him, were only two more victims of his twisted behavior. Mike Vaughn told me he was chilled by the fact that violence was so ingrained in Stephens's nature, he'd thought nothing of smacking around his own mother.

Mike found out that the spark for that day's mayhem had been when Stephens's father discovered the cache of hand grenades and firearms he had been storing at their house—Stephens had been using his parents' suburban split-level as his personal armory. Through magazine ads, Stephens had ordered the parts needed to make a fully automated MAC-10-type submachine gun and live hand grenades. Since he obviously couldn't transact his mail-order business from his back-country hideout, he had given out his parents' Valley Street address as casually as a mechanic purchasing tools.

There are a lot of misconceptions regarding the laws covering ownership of military weapons such as machine guns and hand grenades. The federal statutes can be confusing about who's entitled to legally own such weapons. For years the only governing principle was the famous language of the Second Amendment of the U.S. Constitution: *A well regulated militia being necessary to the security of a free State, the right of the People to keep and bear arms, shall not be infringed.* Prior to

1934, any individual in the United States could own or possess any type of weapon his or her heart desired, be it a tank or 50-caliber machine gun or even a howitzer artillery cannon.

It wasn't until Prohibition-era gangsters like Al Capone, John Dillinger, Baby Face Nelson, and Machine Gun Kelly made headlines by using the Thompson submachine gun to kill both their rivals and the police indiscriminately that the feds realized the law had to change. In 1934 Congress passed the National Firearms Act, restricting ownership of the most high-powered weapons, including machine guns, silencers, short-barreled rifles, and shotguns, and explosive devices such as bombs and hand grenades.

These weapons were not banned outright; they could be owned by law-abiding citizens willing to register them. Congress attached a tax to the regulations, and enforcement of the law was given to the Bureau of Alcohol, Tobacco and Firearms (still known in those days as the Alcohol Tax Unit, or ATU).

Like Frank Nitti or John Dillinger, Mark Stephens was precisely the type of criminal the law was designed to restrict. There was no way he would be able to legally buy the machine guns or hand grenades he desired. Even if he were able to pass the federal guidelines for ownership of an NFA-restricted weapon and had the money to pay the transfer tax, the state of California was one jurisdiction in which ownership of these types of weapons was outright prohibited.

Still, like a lot of modern-day gunmen, Stephens was clever enough to figure out the flaws and loopholes in the system. He didn't have to look far to find the means to build his arsenal.

The guide to ownership by extralegal means could be found in the back pages of a multitude of gun-enthusiast publications. Dozens of unscrupulous gun dealers place advertisements, ducking the gun laws by selling what they describe as "parts" or "legal Title 1–type firearms" that can be converted into fully automatic machine guns with a twist here and a turn there. These unscrupulous dealers keep ATF agents running from one end of the country to the other.

Mark Stephens opted to go the gun-kit route. That meant he'd buy all the separate parts he needed through the mail, then assemble them into an illegal automatic firearm. Such kits contain "flats"—pieces of metal cut, drilled, and notched so that when they are properly bent and welded, they make a receiver for a MAC-10- or MAC-11-type machine gun. Detailed instructions are even furnished, so a less than intelligent barrel sucker can do the assembly. The only real hitch is the welding. But even a half-assed welder could complete the receiver with few problems, and Stephens had strong-armed the services of an expert welder in Kevin. With his assistance, Stephens was able to order and build multiple machine guns.

As for his stockpile of hand grenades, they were similarly easy to acquire. Grenade shells can be purchased through hundreds of vendors. The empty shells come with a hole in the bottom that the purchaser has to plug himself. The most popular way to do this is to weld it closed. But I've also seen them thread-tapped and screwed. The shell is then filled with an explosive, usually a low-explosive material such as black or smokeless powder. Finally, a screw-in fuse is inserted. The most desirable fuse, but hardest to come by, is a regular hand-grenade fuse. Some foolhardy individuals choose to use fuses intended for smoke grenades, gas grenades, or practice grenades. These fuses are not as reliable as the standard military grenade fuse, and the delay is unpredictable, while a standard grenade fuse has about a five-second delay. Practice, smoke, gas, and other fuses usually go off in two to three seconds, meaning you need to get rid of them pretty damn quick after the spoon flies off.

For Mark Stephens's parents, the discovery of the hand grenades right under their roof was the last straw. They'd been afraid to confront their renegade druggie about his comings and goings, but Stephens's father finally understood that the illegal weapons he'd found were a disaster in the making. They could only lead to murder.

"You get those hand grenades out of my house," Stephens's father fumed on the day of the assault. "Mark, I don't want those weapons in my home."

Stephens knew his father was afraid of him, but he also knew his father meant business on this one. He would have to find a new place to stash his weapons.

After witnessing the assault, Mike Vaughn asked me to come meet with Mark Stephens's parents.

I knew that with Chuck Pratt in charge of the Metro Group,

I had a better chance to get the green light and face off with Stephens. I wanted as much information as I could get about what that face-off would entail. In case anything happened to me up on that mountaintop, I wanted another ATF agent to know what I had already learned about Stephens, so I picked up Wayne Morrison, and we hooked up with Mike Vaughn at his house in Rancho Cucamonga. All we had to do was to walk across the street to the Stephenses' home.

"Mike," I said, "I'm gonna get a federal warrant for Stephens's arrest. We're going to end up taking him down in the hills. I want to get as much information from his parents as I can in reference to his violence and what type of weapons we might be looking at."

Mike said that he got along with Stephens's parents quite well and that they were invariably friendly. They were typical suburbanites—conservative, financially successful, and well regarded in their neighborhood. It's normally next to impossible to get a criminal's folks to turn cooperators—parental bonds being parental bonds, after all—but Mike told me that they were deathly afraid of their son. He'd knocked his father and mother around pretty bad and had threatened to kill them on more than one occasion, Mike said.

We approached the Stephens home and rang the bell. It was a picture-perfect Rancho Cucamonga home, a two-story white stucco house with a manicured lawn and a pool out back. *Typical slice of the middle-American dream,* I thought. I rang the bell again and then had a chilling thought—what if Stephens had done away with his parents? What if he were about to open the front door? I nonchalantly slid my palm down toward my gun.

The double bolt unlocked from the inside, and the door swung open. There stood a clean-cut gentleman in his fifties, about six feet tall, square-jawed, salt and pepper in his hair. He smiled right away when he saw his neighbor. "Hi, Mike," he said.

Mike stepped up. "Hi, Russell," he said. "These guys are friends of mine. This is Special Agent Bill Queen and Special Agent Wayne Morrison with the Bureau of Alcohol, Tobacco and Firearms. They were hoping to talk with you about Mark."

Russell's face tightened a bit at the mention of his son's name. But he quickly invited us into the front hall, then gestured to the living room. "Please have a seat," he said.

Mark's mother, Geri, soon joined us. We all sat down and got to know a bit about one another. Russell was a corporate salesman, well spoken and polite; Geri was a homemaker who kept a neat, nicely furnished home.

After the introductions, I cut to the chase. "I don't want to upset you folks too much, but as you probably know, Mark's been creating quite an uproar around the Inland area," I said. "He's shot up a couple of places with a machine gun and assaulted a few people. He's got outstanding warrants from a bunch of local police departments, but it's a federal matter now. ATF is interested in Mark because of the machine-gun stuff and what we've learned recently about his being in possession of hand grenades."

Neither Russell nor Geri seemed surprised by what I'd said. I went on, "We also know that he is growing marijuana in the San Bernardino Mountains on federal land. The reason I'm here is to find out if there may be a way of taking him into custody without using violence."

Geri was concerned and said that she hoped her son would give up without a fight. She said he had been living in the mountains for a few years and that his problems had been increasing. She said she thought that his psychological problems stemmed from drugs. He wasn't really a bad boy, but when he was on drugs, he went crazy.

I asked about the hand grenades, and Russell cleared his throat, noticeably upset. He said he'd been stunned when he found out that Mark had the grenades in the house. He had immediately confronted his son and told him to get rid of them.

"So you did see the grenades?" I asked.

"Oh, yes," he responded, "and I made him get them out of the house."

I asked when Mark might come down out of the hills again, and they both said that he came and went at different times, usually on a Thursday or Friday. But his movements were completely erratic and unpredictable.

"He doesn't say when he'll be back, and he usually doesn't say when he's leaving," Russell said. "It's been like that for some time now, so it would be a guess as to when he might be back."

Geri began pleading with us. "You won't hurt him? You won't hurt him when you arrest him?"

"No, ma'am, I'll try not to hurt him."

I looked at Russell and asked what I could expect when I encountered his son.

Russell's expression became stern. "Agent Queen, you better be ready for anything."

"Do you think he'll shoot?"

"You better be ready for anything," Russell repeated. "He'll fight you. He'll shoot you. If you're not careful, I have no doubt he'll kill you."

"What other types of guns does Mark have?"

Russell seemed embarrassed by what he'd seen his son carrying. He'd seen Mark with some type of pistol, he said, a big handgun—either a 9mm or a .45. He thought Mark always had that handgun on his person.

We ended the interview. "Thank you for your time and cooperation. You'll give me or Mike a call if Mark does come home?" I asked.

Geri seemed a bit reluctant, or perhaps afraid, but Russell said that if he could get to a phone without Mark seeing him, he'd definitely tip us off.

Nine

I was typing up 3270s from the Sergeant and Pajack under-cover deal when I got a call from Bill Kendrick, the Mont-clair detective who'd first warned me about Mark Stephens.

"Queen, better get down here."

"Why, what's up?"

"Stephens is here in Montclair."

"You saw him?"

"We got a victim in one of our black-and-whites. She's scared to death and saying that Stephens was just at her house looking for her. He's on foot, so he can't be far. We've got our patrol units searching the neighborhood for him right now."

"Is he armed?" I asked, knowing what the answer would be.

"With at least one handgun."

I told Detective Kendrick I would be right there. For the first time, I had real-time intel that Stephens was at a fixed location. He was somewhere in the city of Montclair, or at least nearby.

The only hitch was traffic. I was at my desk at L.A. Metro, and I knew I would need a helicopter to get from downtown to the Inland Empire. The freeways around Los Angeles are some of the best and biggest in the United States, but there are more cars in L.A. than in any other city in the country. Two or six lanes wide, if you catch a bad break, you're going to be rolling along at thirty-five miles an hour along with a million other frustrated drivers. Doesn't make much difference what time of the day it is.

I wanted Stephens bad, like a lot of other cops. But for me it was becoming an obsession. The case was taking a toll on my home life. My wife, Mary, was also in law enforcement; she was a U.S. Customs agent working in Riverside, California, and we lived in a beautiful home in Corona. While I was out doing undercover operations and gathering intel on Stephens, Mary was busy chasing dope smugglers in the desert areas of Riverside and San Bernardino. At night I would listen to her stories about the smugglers, and I'd tell her about Mark Stephens and the other cases I was involved in. But that was where our career similarities ended. I drove fast G-rides and raced around on a Harley motorcycle. Mary was much more civilized and, to my view, less enthusiastic about putting the bad guys in jail. She tended to follow the admin line, something I could never bring myself to do.

Mary was becoming increasingly put off by my hours. She hated that I would get up at three in the morning and leave her not knowing when she would see me again. She was baffled that I was able to stay focused enough to put together one significant case after another. And she could never understand how single-minded and obsessive I could become about a case, especially Mark Stephens. The more I focused on the Stephens investigation, the more it seemed to piss her off.

I hit the freeway and headed to Montclair, throwing caution and legal niceties to the wind. Swerving lanes, gunning my Mustang down the shoulder, I ran to the Inland Empire, defying the California Highway Patrol and other well-meaning traffic cops.

And then I hit the gas.

Being able to handle a car at high speeds seemed to come naturally to me. I must have picked it up from my dad, who was noted as one of the best, if not the best, driver ATF had back in the revenuer days. While most ATF agents drove the standard-issue four-door police cars, my dad was too much of a speed freak for that. He always drove seized muscle cars with big block engines, like GTOs and Chevelle Super Sports.

The one I remember best was a seized 1964 R-model Ford Galaxy. It had a 427-cubic-inch engine with two four-barrel carburetors and a four-speed shifter. The wheels on the back had been modified so he could run a set of Grand National racing tires. Everybody in the Carolinas called that Ford the Batmobile.

In the early seventies, as a young guy, I felt that hot-rod bug in my blood. After Vietnam, I raced stock cars for two years in NASCAR's Limited Late Model Sportsman Division. Racing Limited Sportsmen, I didn't have a pit crew, just a couple of friends, Tom Smith and Harold Walls, who enjoyed racing as much as I did. Most people don't realize that racers are operating on the very edge of being out of control all the time. That means if the least little thing goes wrong, you cross over the thin line of control and are at the mercy of high-speed dynamics. I found out pretty quick that figuring out this line needed a lot of attention if I was going to be competitive. Being loose or tight really did mean something. Jacking weight in and out, wedge, tire pressure, composition, and springs were only the tip of the iceberg. I also found out that racing requires a lot of money.

Bill Blair and the High Point Police Department didn't pay enough to support a race car, and although I consistently ran in the top five on my circuit, my career as a driver was short-lived. Racing one night at Caraway, I spun my car off the track. A driver behind me made the mistake of taking a low track, trying to avoid my spinning car. He hit me in the side, nearly splitting my car in half, and I ended up at the hospital. I was lucky I didn't die on the track.

Within thirty minutes, I'd hooked up with Kendrick and a couple of patrolmen who were searching Montclair for Stephens. By now I knew of several locations where Stephens might attempt to hide out. He could hole up with at least two marijuana dealers working for him in Montclair or two other associates not far from the area.

I started running from location to location till I found myself in the city of Ontario. I didn't think much about going from city to city or county to county; my badge has a big U.S. on it, and jurisdictions didn't factor in. In California, all police officers have law enforcement authority statewide. Protocol dictates that jurisdictions notify one another, if possible, when crossing county or city lines, but I didn't have time for that today.

I rolled into the industrial area where Kevin's welding shop was located. I'd been by Kevin's shop enough in my hunt for Stephens that at this point all the neighbors knew who I was. Given Kevin's obvious fear of his former friend, I felt most of the neighbors would provide me with better information than Kevin would on the subject of Mark Stephens.

I parked my Mustang and walked to a neighbor's open bay door. I didn't even have to ask a question. The neighbor, a mechanic, looked stone-faced. He spoke in a hushed tone. "I saw your boy walk into Kevin's a couple of minutes ago."

With no radio and no backup, I pulled my pistol and headed for Kevin's front door. What the neighbor hadn't bothered to mention was that he'd already called the Ontario Police Department and they had dispatched black-and-whites to Kevin's with the advisory: *Be on the lookout for Mark Stephens. White male, late thirties. Wanted by several jurisdictions. Numerous felony assault charges. Should be considered armed and dangerous.*

I cautiously entered Kevin's welding shop, listening closely with each step. I was breathing fast, but I tried to keep quiet.

What was waiting for me? Was I walking right into an ambush? I felt my pulse begin to race with each step. In the open area of his shop, Kevin stood by himself. I positioned myself out of sight behind the door, then called out Kevin's name.

When Kevin recognized me, he looked frightened—too frightened to speak. He made a gesture toward the open bay door, notifying me that Stephens had just exited. I slipped back the way I had come.

Stephens had likely seen my approach and made his getaway.

I wanted to ask Kevin what type of gun Stephens was carrying, but I was in too much of a hurry. I exited the shop and headed toward the railroad tracks north of the industrial complex.

It wasn't long before I saw Stephens about two hundred yards ahead, running west on the tracks.

My heart was pounding hard. It was my first glimpse of Stephens in the flesh. I couldn't see his face, but the very image of my quarry had the adrenaline pumping through my system. I broke into a sprint. Running hard, I stayed close by the industrial buildings, trying to use them as cover so Stephens wouldn't see me.

I was gaining ground on him when, unbeknownst to me, a Good Samaritan spotted me running behind his shop with my gun drawn. He darted inside and dialed 911. *White male, blue jeans, black shirt, tennis shoes, seen running behind the building in the industrial park* was the call that came in to the Ontario Police Department.

I had closed the gap on Stephens to the point where I would have to make a decision about confronting him. I knew that if I shouted for him to freeze, he would unhesitatingly open fire on me. I was going through the scenarios of a shoot-out when I heard a loud, authoritative voice behind me.

"Police! Freeze! Drop the weapon!"

I almost pissed myself. Still, my years on the job had honed my cop instincts: I knew better than to turn around with my gun in hand. I stopped dead in my tracks and, with my back still to the officer, began to yell: "I'm a cop! I'm a cop!"

The response was loud and instantaneous: "Drop your weapon *now*!"

Moving as slowly as possible, I lowered my handgun to the ground.

"Hands up! Hands *up*!"

I knew I could keep yelling "cop!" all day and it wouldn't make any difference. In the corner of my vision, I could see the figure of Mark Stephens running along the rail tracks, disappearing from sight. A wave of anger surged through me as I realized I had missed my best shot to catch him away from his mountain hideout.

The officer's partner moved up close beside me. He had been covering me from my flank, and I hadn't even seen him. One twitch on my part and this guy might have blown me away.

Both OPD officers moved in while I kept announcing, now in a quieter voice, "I'm a cop, guys. I'm a cop. I'm a special agent with ATF."

The first officer commanded me to keep my hands up and move away from my firearm. I took three steps to the left. After the officer's partner had picked up my firearm, he could see that the gun had a U.S. badge stamped on the side of it. They commanded me to put my hands on top of my head and interlace my fingers.

"Turn around! Slowly," the first officer said.

I turned around, and he proceeded to grab my hands and firmly mash my fingers together. He patted me down and removed my identification from my pocket. Only after they'd opened it and studied the creds displaying SPECIAL AGENT WILLIAM QUEEN, BUREAU OF ALCOHOL, TOBACCO AND FIRE-ARMS did the two patrolmen start to listen to me.

"Look, fellas, I was chasing Mark Stephens," I said. "He was right up there on the tracks. Probably has a machine gun on him."

Of course they'd heard of Mark Stephens; he was one of the OPD's more notorious felony warrants.

"It would be nice if you guys called for some backup and we tried to find him," I said. "He should be considered armed and dangerous. He just scared the bejesus out of some chick in Montclair and will probably be headed for the Rancho Cuca-monga area to get away."

I calculated that Stephens could be just a few blocks away at most. If he was still traveling on foot, he couldn't be out of the Ontario area.

But I'd lost the edge now. I would have to make my way back

to my car, which was parked a good three or four blocks away, by Kevin's shop. The OPD cops were a couple of blocks from their own black-and-white. The only chance we had of catching Stephens was to use the Ontario police radio.

The two cops called in assistance. A few more black-and-whites did a good job cordoning off the area. But it was an exercise in futility. Stephens had vanished. I kept cursing to myself over and over, again realizing that my best chance of apprehending him had slipped through my fingers. At least I was lucky I hadn't gotten my ass shot by these patrol guys mistaking me—a white male in his thirties, openly carrying a gun—for Mark Stephens.

The patrol sergeant on the scene wanted to know why I hadn't notified Ontario PD about the operation in advance.

"When exactly was I supposed to stop my pursuit to call you guys?" I asked the patrol sergeant.

I knew where he was coming from. Protocol was protocol. But that didn't change the fact that because of the confusion, Stephens was still running the streets, free to threaten their community.

Pissed at the OPD, pissed at myself, I rolled back to the Montclair Police Department, planning to hook up with Bill Kendrick and his fellow detectives and let them know what had transpired.

Still, I knew Stephens would be heading for the hills, and I thought there might be one more chance to cut him off before he made his ascent. I pulled a U-turn and headed east on the San

Bernardino Freeway, toward Rancho Cucamonga. I wanted to hit the gas, but there was little sense in gunning it over sixty. The way my luck was going today, I'd probably get jammed by some local guy and wind up with a speeding ticket.

There were several locations I could set up on. Stephens's parents' house, the nearby convenience store, or somewhere on his trail back to the mountains. I went for the road that led to the wash. I had a good hiding place for my G-ride, on the south side of Baseline Road in the scrub brush, where no one could see the red Mustang.

I never sat in my car when I was on a stakeout. There were just too many stories of cops getting killed that way. It was always my practice to get out and wait someplace nearby. I walked across the street to the access road, found my hiding place in some brush, and settled in for the wait. I waited and waited on the access road. The sun began to set, and I resigned myself to the realization that Stephens had slipped past me. I wasn't going to be locking him up, at least not tonight.

I did my regular routine the following morning. I was up at three A.M. and heading downtown. I parked my G-ride and was in the gym before dawn. I worked out alone that morning, replaying in my mind's eye what had happened the night before. Stephens's luck was incredible, and mine was so awful. Something had to change in this equation.

I made it to the office around seven A.M. feeling drained. I had hung out till past dark on the access road, so by the time I had gotten home and taken care of what was left of my personal life, it was late. I decided to curl up under my desk and catch a few minutes of rest.

Boom. It was as if the lights had gone out. I didn't wake up until I was nudged by Chuck Pratt's black shoe. "What in the hell are you doing, Queen?"

I couldn't believe I had fallen into such a deep sleep. I guess telling him that I had dropped something and was looking for it wasn't going to fly.

"Shit, I just lay down for a moment. I guess I fell asleep."

Pratt kept staring at me, wanting an explanation.

"I was out chasing Stephens around Ontario last night," I said.

"Chasing Stephens? Who was with you?"

"No one."

I told him a half-truth, that the Ontario Police Department and the Montclair PD had backed me for a while. I said I hadn't gotten any help from the ATF guys because I hadn't wanted to keep them on a stakeout that might come to nothing.

Pratt stared at me some more. "Stop doing that, Queen," he said.

I got up and followed him to his office. "You want to hear what Stephens did yesterday?"

Pratt knew I was going to push him again about going up in the hills. "No, I don't actually."

"The son of a bitch was waving his gun at people in Montclair. Threatening to shoot folks. I got a call from the PD and ended up chasing him around the area till Ontario cops jammed me. I guess I was lucky some PD cop didn't shoot me."

"What?" Pratt said. "Who jammed you?"

"Ontario PD. Somebody saw me with my gun out chasing Stephens and called the cops."

"Queen, are you trying to tell me you pulled your *gun* on Stephens?" Pratt asked. Drawing a gun on anyone is considered use of force and has to be documented in an incident report.

"No, I just had it out. I couldn't run with it sticking in my waistband, so I had it in my hand. Chuck, I didn't draw my gun in the line of duty. I had it in my hand while trying to run Stephens down."

I knew it wouldn't be a good time to talk to Pratt any further. I cut my losses and started to head back to my desk.

"Queen, get back here!" Pratt called. I shuffled back into his office. "You're gonna be working backup for a while."

Ten

reg Nottingham was a detective for the Ontario Police Department. A few months back, we'd hooked up on a joint ATF-OPD operation targeting white-power hate groups in the Inland Empire. I had been working undercover, riding a Harley-Davidson and hanging out with neo-Nazis and the Aryan Nations in the Ontario and Chino area. ATF got involved in these kinds of cases because of the hate groups' propensity for violence and their drug and gun running in the Inland Empire.

A few days after my aborted chase of Stephens, I was at the Ontario Police Department to smooth things over with OPD brass after the patrolmen had jammed me up. I asked Greg Nottingham about his greatest threat in the area.

"It's a toss-up between the Skinheads and Mark Stephens," Greg said.

I already knew Stephens was scaring the shit out of people. But while he was a ticking time bomb, this group of vile racists calling themselves the Ontario Skinheads had recently been committing their own acts of violence; there had been a new spate of crimes linked to them in recent weeks. Cops knew the Ontario Skinheads were responsible for a number of assaults in the area, mainly against blacks. The attacks hadn't occurred because the victims were confronting the Skinheads, or because of drug deals gone bad. No, the Skinheads were attacking blacks at random simply because of their skin color.

I listened to Greg talking about how threatening the Skins were, how they were dealing drugs and were heavy into guns. He said the Ontario PD could really use some help from the feds.

"Hey," I said to him, "I got a Harley, I got a country accent, I'm from the South. You know I can play that Knights of the KKK shit pretty good. Let's run a UC operation in on 'em."

"Sounds like a great idea to me," Greg said.

A few days later, I was at my desk downtown when I got a call from Greg. He asked if I was serious about running an undercover operation on the Ontario Skinheads.

"You bet I am," I told him.

"Well, Agent Queen, it's your lucky day. I got a guy who can take you in."

Bill Queen and his father, Bill Queen, Sr., who was a Washington, D.C., park policeman at the time. Bill would soon follow in his dad's footsteps.

Bill and his twin brother, Jimmy (right), in high school. They both reported to boot camp two weeks after they graduated.

At twenty-four, Bill became a local cop in High Point, North Carolina—his first job after Vietnam.

Bill, on the firing range at the ATF academy when he was training to be an agent.

Bill, wearing full camouflage during a training exercise with the Special Forces.

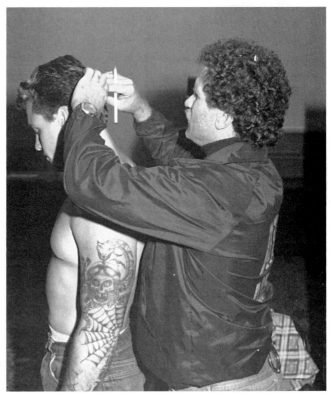

While processing an arrested suspect into custody, Bill looks at the skinhead tattoo on his scalp. The man was later convicted of drug and gun charges.

The San Bernardino Mountains, shot from a helicopter.

Bill (left) gets his gear together as he prepares to go into the mountains and face Mark Stephens.

The team that apprehended Mark Stephens.

Mark Stephens, soon after his arrest.

Lanny Royer, standing in Stephens's marijuana fields. Some marijuana plants reached twelve feet high.

A helicopter piloted by Tom Federoff tries to angle into an area where Bill and his colleagues can jump on board.

Bill, soon after the shootout.

"Who's this?"

"He's a bad guy out here trying to work off a beef. He said we can buy guns, dope, stolen merchandise. You name it—they're into it."

"Greg, your timing is impeccable," I said. I had just finished typing up paperwork requesting that ATF open an investigation into the Skinheads. But I would need to put in a few more hours of paper: requests for federal money, electronic surveillance equipment, sufficient ATF backup on the scene.

"I just love it," I told Greg. "The paperwork, I mean."

I said I wanted to meet the informant as soon as it could be arranged. Greg set up the meeting for that very afternoon.

Although skinheads are normally a young crowd, usually in their teens and early twenties, hate groups such as the KKK, neo-Nazis, and Ontario Skinheads are always recruiting new members. The fact that I was a good ten years older than their oldest member probably wouldn't be a major stumbling block.

Ontario is roughly forty miles east of the Los Angeles city limits. To get down to the meet, I would drive through Montclair, Pomona, Upland, and Fontana—the hunting grounds for Mark Stephens. I found myself wondering what Stephens was up to at that moment, and how close I might be to him.

I rolled into the parking lot at the Ontario Police Department and met Greg Nottingham standing outside. We were both excited about kicking off the UC operation. Greg was telling me about a vicious attack on a young black male that had made the papers in Ontario. No one had been arrested, but the crime was believed to be the work of the Ontario Skinheads. The publicity meant we could count on all the administrative support we needed.

The CI was waiting for us inside. He was a white guy in his early twenties, with an unkempt look, a few cheap tattoos, and telltale short-clipped hair. He looked like he was a pretty heavy drug abuser, and I realized that getting an intro to a violent group from this guy was going to be risky business.

After we'd talked with the CI for a while about what was going on at the Skinheads' clubhouse, Greg grabbed him by the shoulder and stared hard into his eyes. "If you piss backwards on us," he said, "if Billy gets hurt because of you, I'll make you pay for the rest of your life, you got that?"

Greg is a giant of a man, standing about six-four, at 250 pounds, and the CI was instantly agreeable.

"No problem, guys," he stammered. "I swear, no problem."

We took a ride by the clubhouse. Nothing major, just an intel-gathering run to see what was going on. The clubhouse was located in a modest section of Ontario. It was an unassuming house. No one seemed to be home at the time.

From the backseat, the CI said, "Oh, yeah. They're in there, all right. They keep everything locked down so no one will know what the fuck they're up to."

A few days later, I rode my Harley-Davidson Super Glide to the Ontario Police Department and met up with Greg, the CI, and a backup team comprised of cops from the OPD and agents from ATF. It was time to make our first undercover contact with the Skinheads. No buys, no recordings, no arrests, only an intro. The CI would drive his truck, and I would follow him on my bike. The CI had indicated that the Skinheads were into motorcycles, especially Harleys, and that it would make a good impression if I showed up on my hog. A simple operation, not too much danger—at least that was what I wanted to believe. I wanted ATF to think so, too, because risky business isn't looked upon favorably by a lot of the brass at ATF.

After a quick brief at the PD, we headed out. I rolled up in front of the clubhouse behind the CI's truck. Today there were a couple of guys out front. They stared at me on the Harley and immediately took to me. When I got off the bike, we struck up a conversation about motorcycles.

The CI walked back to them and introduced me as one of his friends, Billy St. John. We stood there talking about the bike for a couple more minutes, then we went into the clubhouse. I guess I thought there would be more political rhetoric and signs of self-promotion. But the inside of the house was pretty much normal. There were girls and guys sitting around watching TV. The guys all had their shirts off, proudly displaying their skinhead markings: tattoos of swastikas and SS insignia, Nazi paraphernalia, Celtic crosses, and other white-power signs. There were a lot of prison-pumped physiques in that room. Most of the guys had their hair trimmed close with a number-two clippers.

The girls were acting like groupies backstage at some punk-rock concert. The CI asked one of the skinnier Skinheads where the head pooh-bah was. The skinny guy went to a door off the living room and knocked. A voice from inside answered, "Yo, come on in."

When the door opened, I saw a large, heavily tattooed individual inside the room with a girl. They were putting their clothes on. It looked like they'd just been having sex.

The big guy exited the room, buttoning his shirt. His name was Robert. The CI introduced me, muttering that I was a real cool guy and that I had a lot of money. Then the CI told Robert that I was from North Carolina and was, like, a Grand Dragon in the KKK back there. Robert shook my hand forcefully. He said I was welcome at their place anytime. He was more businesslike than I would have expected. He had a commanding presence, and everyone treated him with great deference.

The CI and I hung around for a few minutes and then left, telling the group that we'd be back later. One of the Skinheads in the living room lit a joint and offered it to the CI. He took a long hit and then offered it to me.

I glared furiously, then caught myself. "Thanks," I said. "But I'm already as high as I can get today."

When we got outside and well out of earshot, I turned to the CI. "Motherfucker, you ever do that again on a deal, and I'll have your ass."

He knew he had made a bad mistake. "Okay, man," he said. Nothing else needed to be said.

My next trip to the Skinhead clubhouse would reveal exactly how sick this group of people really was. The plan was to send our CI back to set up a dope deal. He was instructed to tell the Skins that I wanted to buy quantities of cocaine and perhaps grass.

On my way home that night, I again started thinking about Mark Stephens. I decided I'd drive by Stephens's parents' house in Rancho Cucamonga to see if I could spot something, although I wasn't quite sure what I'd do if I ran into Stephens. I didn't have an arrest warrant for him, and if he was there, I'd probably catch him with a machine gun. He would no doubt pull out on me, and I'd end up in a gunfight, me with my six-shooter wheel gun and Stephens with a thirty-round MAC-10. I remembered how, when I was a kid, my dad and his fellow agents would carry Thompson submachine guns. They also carried dynamite and TNT and det cord in the trunks of their cars. Those old boys were never outgunned.

It seemed to me that some of the brass in ATF would rather arm us street agents with Daisy BB guns. Restraint was always the order of the day. Despite what people may believe, during the infamous standoff in Waco, Texas, ATF faced a slew of machine guns, firearms as powerful as 50-caliber automatics, and explosive devices, and not one ATF agent carried a machine gun into the operation. I remember the ATF press agent saying on TV, "We were simply outgunned," and the ATF brass flat-out denied it. But it was the truth. Even today ATF's special response teams (SRTs) are some of the most well-trained and proficient units in the federal system, but they are allowed to carry only a three-round-burst firearm.

With visions of being completely outgunned, I rolled onto Valley Street in Rancho Cucamonga. It was still dark, but I could see a shadowy figure standing in the front yard. It was definitely a man. *Holy shit,* I thought. *It's him.* I drove past, trying not to give myself away.

What now? I may not have had a federal warrant, but I knew there were local warrants out for his arrest. I could call for backup and approach. But I didn't know for sure whether it was Stephens. I drove my Mustang out of sight so he wouldn't see me turning around. I made the U-turn, then got ready to make another pass by the house.

I reached down and pulled my revolver from the holster. I approached Stephens's house. Now no one was standing out front.

Then, to my surprise, a male figure appeared right in front of my car, walking down the street. It was definitely the same person who had been standing in the yard. My headlights illuminated the man from behind, and I got a good look at him. White male, about six feet tall, powerful build.

This has to be Mark Stephens, I told myself. I decided to follow him for a while. As much as I wanted to collar him, I didn't want to get into a confrontation with him, considering the potential for a fatal shoot-out. *If it goes upside down,* I thought, *the first thing ATF will want to know is why I was in front of the Stephens residence with no backup.* In fact, why was I on the scene in the first place?

But I didn't want to let him go. I got on the radio. "ATF," I said. "This is Queen."

Nothing.

"ATF! This is Queen."

Still nothing.

There was no chance of calling in backup—nobody was there to answer the radio at this time in the evening. I would have to find another way to follow him. Passing by him again would tip him off to the fact that I was tailing him. I pulled out of sight and looked for an inconspicuous place to hide my G-ride. I thought I'd pull in to a driveway and act like I lived in that house.

No. It was too quiet and upscale a neighborhood. Someone was sure to call the cops on me. I decided to park on a cross street another block down. I cut my lights, pulled onto the next cross street, and turned my car around. Streetlights lit up the area, including my Mustang. I slid down as low as I could in the seat, eyes peering just over the dash. Maybe I would see him with an open gun. That would give me all the probable cause I needed with the brass.

I flicked the radio back on. I figured I'd try CLEMARS, a common law enforcement radio frequency, and see if I could get a local to back me up. If they couldn't send backup, one of the locals could pull a routine stop on the guy.

I waited in the car for the guy to approach on foot, but I didn't want to start my car for fear of giving myself away. Three minutes passed. Then five. He should have made it to the cross street by now. Shit, where was he?

My mind started to play tricks on me. What if he'd spotted me and was trying to flank me right now? What if he'd seen my whole route and watched me pulling my Mustang onto the cross street? What if he had his machine gun already drawn?

No way was I going to be Mark Stephens's next victim. I started the car and gunned the engine. I thought I caught sight of the figure momentarily, but then he disappeared in the shadows. If Stephens was the least bit suspicious, then he had to know I was surveilling him. I left Rancho Cucamonga and headed home to my house in Corona.

The next morning I woke up to the roar of tanker planes dive-bombing the neighborhood. I lived across from the Chino Hills State Park, and the park was on fire. Wildfires were always breaking out in the desert climate. If there was a drought, then the wildfires raged out of control and made the national news.

I had a close-up view of the odd-looking aircraft dumping red fire retardant on the hill behind my house. I'd seen the planes many times on the news, and I'd watched as neighborhoods and tens of thousands of acres in Southern California went up in flames, occasionally taking human lives with them. Firestorms are an incredible phenomenon to see up close. I wanted to hang out at my house and watch the dive-bombing, but I had an undercover buy lined up for that evening at the Ontario Skinheads' clubhouse.

With the planes buzzing overhead, I headed for downtown L.A. Ordinarily, I took the back roads, but not today. The fire department owned the roads. I hit the 91 freeway. Traffic never seemed to help my attitude. By the time I got to work, I felt like someone had licked all the red off my candy.

Around nine A.M. I got a call from Detective Greg Nottingham. He said the CI had told him that besides the prearranged dope buy, there was another Skinhead at the house who was looking to sell a gun. All we needed were a few more UC dollars and we'd be killing two birds with one stone. I got the paperwork done, then ran around the office looking for volunteers to back that night's deal.

With that office full of go-getters, it wasn't too much of a surprise to find that everybody was either out on an undercover deal of his own or backing someone else's deal. Howard Sanders was my only ATF backup for this night, besides the cops from the OPD.

On undercover deals, you can have one backup or twenty. Doesn't make much difference; it's up to the UC to save his own ass. Backup guys rarely rescue an undercover. If things go bad, your backup is really just the first responder on the scene to clean up the bloody mess.

Howard was a friend of mine and never seemed to mind doing backup duties. We arrived at the OPD somewhere around four P.M. I had stopped off to pick up my Harley, and I had a pocketful of ATF money. We could buy guns, dope, and any other illegal shit the Skins might come up with.

I followed the CI's truck again, parking my bike in the front yard. Several Skinheads were out front, and it looked like something unusual was in the works. One of the guys was holding two small kittens, one in each hand. The kittens couldn't have been more than a few weeks old. It was incongruous, seeing such cute little animals in the hands of muscle-bound Skinheads covered in racist tattoos. They weren't exactly the nurturing types. Why would any of these guys give a shit about two little kittens? I didn't have much time to ponder the situation, though.

"Billy, you got here just in time," said one of the Skinheads. We walked into the house and straight through to the back door. Everyone headed into the backyard. Two ferocious-looking pit bulls were running free. Behind me came the guy carrying the two little kittens.

Robert, the boss Skinhead, turned to me and cackled. "Yo, Billy, watch this," he said.

The guy with the two kittens tossed them out in front of him onto the patchy lawn. They landed on their feet, right in front of the pit bulls. In a savage split second, the dogs grabbed the kittens in their massive jaws. I watched in horror as the pit bulls began ripping the kittens apart, blood and intestines and fur flying everywhere. All the Skinheads cheered them on, laughing and commenting in graphic detail on how the kittens were being torn to bits.

It was sickening, and I was pissed. I wanted to smack the shit out of every last one of those sick assholes. But there was nothing I could do. I had to wait it out. We were in the middle of a well-planned undercover op.

The kittens were dead, half eaten. The Ontario Skinheads couldn't wait to line up and get their pictures taken with the pit bulls. The dogs' faces were covered in blood.

I stood there, telling myself, *Just wait, Billy Boy. They'll get theirs soon.*

After the slaughter and the picture taking, we all walked back inside to do business. The boss told one of his underlings to go get the dope, then told me to give the money to one of his underlings.

I had them now; it had gone perfectly. I had three bad guys all participating in the same dope deal. Before I had finished the deal, Skinhead number four showed up with the piece-of-crap shotgun he wanted to sell. And to sweeten the pot, he was toting what looked to be a nice Colt model 1911 .45. He didn't offer the Colt for sale, but that didn't matter. He was part of the dope deal, and getting caught in possession of the .45 would tack on another five years in the joint. But even though the deal was well under way, I still couldn't get the backyard slaughter of those kittens out of my mind.

Three Skinheads down in one dope and gun deal. Two more ops like that and we'd have the entire Ontario Skinhead organization locked up. The Skinheads were only too glad to get their hands on ATF money.

With my southern accent and good-ol'-boy small talk, they looked at me as one of them. Except I had money. None of them ever asked me what I did for a living; I suppose since none of them seemed to have a job, they probably thought I did illegal hustles, like them. Surprisingly, there wasn't any talk about going out to terrorize blacks or Jews, or any white-power rhetoric. In their day-to-day lives, they seemed to be a bunch of loser dropouts looking for some way to make it to hell early.

When I got back to the OPD for the debrief, I was still reeling from the kitten incident. There was a lot of high-fiving and backslapping; everybody was happy with how the dope and gun buy had gone down, but when I told them about the kittens and the pit bulls, the atmosphere sobered. The Ontario cops were as pissed as I was. We told ourselves there was nothing we could have done to prevent the kittens from getting killed, but there was no doubt in anyone's mind what kind of people we were about to lock up.

Though we were preparing the warrants, real names were difficult to come up with. The Skinheads called one another by aliases or street names, and that was all I was ever able to pass on. Only one person seemed to have a car, and the cops were never able to find anyone who had a righteous ID on them.

The stories continued to come into the Ontario Police Department. Bands of young white tattooed men from the neighborhood were still attacking and beating mainly black victims.

We wanted to take down all the Ontario Skinheads in this undercover operation. But how? Trying to push too fast with another dope-and-gun deal would be a huge red flag. I had no choice but to go back in there undercover and hang out and drink beer with the scumbags.

By now they'd loosened up around me, and I started to see them for who they really were: They no longer seemed like regular dropout losers. I began to catch wind of their violent political philosophy. They would talk about blacks incessantly, always calling them "niggers." There were lots of jokes about blacks and Jews, and a lot of talk about how superior we were to them.

These punks were violent racists, and they needed to go to prison. I wanted to round them up and take this operation down. I went back to the clubhouse several more times, buying more guns and dope till I had enough on seven of the members.

Fridays were a big night at the clubhouse. Most of the Skins would be there, hanging out, drinking, and getting high. We planned our takedown for a Friday night, when we knew most of them would be at the house.

Raid night came, and with warrants in hand, ATF and OPD hit the clubhouse with a fury. We stormed in there like military commandos, screaming for everyone to keep their hands where we could see them. With shocked expressions, the Skinheads learned the truth: that Billy St. John, their older KKK associate, was a federal agent.

Something went wrong on this particular Friday, and only four Skinheads we'd drawn warrants on were at the house. We did have names for the three other Skinheads, but no addresses. We'd have to catch up with them when we could find them.

Two weeks after the raid on the Skinheads' clubhouse, my wife, Mary, and I were out for a ride on my Super Glide. It was a gorgeous sunny Saturday afternoon, and I was planning to stop at the Harley-Davidson dealership in Pomona to see about getting some work done on the bike.

The service area for the dealership was behind the showroom. I rode the Super Glide behind the dealership and into the service area. Right in front of me, standing at the counter, were four of the Ontario Skinheads I'd met undercover. Three of the four were the ones we'd drawn up federal warrants for.

The Skinheads immediately recognized me and cursed at me under their breath. I was stuck. There wasn't enough room to turn the bike around and leave, and I didn't want my wife to get caught in the cross fire. I knew from firsthand experience that the Skins almost always carried guns.

There was no other option open to me. I shut my bike off and very calmly pulled my gun on them. "Freeze!" I said. "Keep your hands where I can see 'em."

I told Mary to go find a pay phone and call 911, to tell the operator that a federal agent needed assistance. I held the four Skinheads against the wall and waited for the Pomona black-and-whites.

Eleven

Monday morning, with all seven of the Skinheads we'd targeted behind bars, I felt emboldened. I went straight to Chuck Pratt's office to push him again on the mountain-man operation.

"So no matter how many lives Stephens might destroy, no matter how many communities he terrorizes, no matter how many hand grenades and machine guns he possesses, we aren't going after him? Is that what you're telling me, Chuck?"

He shrugged. It wasn't his call to make. "Skopeck said you're not going up in the hills, and that's that," he said. "Two SWAT teams have already tried and failed. What makes you think you're the one who can get him in his own backyard?"

"Because Wayne and I are both Special Forces soldiers—you know that, Chuck. Come on, give me a break. I can go get this guy by myself, all right? I don't need no SWAT team."

"I believe you," Pratt said, "but if I were to tell you it was okay to go up there, I might as well go on my house-hunting trip to Iceberg, North Dakota."

"So what can we do about this guy?"

Pratt said Skopeck was willing to meet me halfway. "You can take somebody with you and set up on Stephens's trail. You know he's probably coming out of the hills on a Thursday or Friday, right? So give it a shot. Hell, if you sit there long enough, you're bound to catch him."

"I ought to go up and set fire to the hills and smoke him out," I said, half laughing. But I knew I was at a dead end. I could keep chasing Stephens around the streets of Southern California, or go set up on the trail.

I left Pratt's office and called up Wayne Morrison. "Wayne, how'd you like to take a few days, all expenses paid, and just lay out in the sun?"

"There will be bikini-clad women, I assume."

"Yeah. You'll just be beside yourself."

I told Wayne that Pratt and Skopeck had given us the green light to set up on Stephens's trail. "I'll hook up with you when I get the details down."

Wayne was game for anything. He and I would take on an army of bad guys anytime, anyplace.

Who knows? I thought. We could catch him coming out of the hills. If we were going to give it a shot, we'd better be ready for his firepower. I knew that any confrontation with Stephens could be deadly. I also knew that, within the parameters of federal regulations, there was no way I was going to get outgunned. I'd match anything Stephens could throw my way. I had an AR-15, and I'd managed to weasel a Colt scope out of Pratt that fit the AR. I tried to convince myself that one AR-15 equaled one MAC-10.

I told Wayne to meet me after work for a drink at the Pomona Valley Mining Company, a little restaurant and bar that sits on top of a hill overlooking the 10 freeway and the Pomona Valley area. We met at about six P.M., and I filled him in on the sunbathing trip.

We watched the cars crawl bumper-to-bumper on the freeway, never breaking twenty miles an hour. Wayne told me he'd already figured that this wouldn't be some Malibu Beach stakeout. But he was as gung ho as I was to head into the hills, and he wasn't too enthused about settling for anything short of that.

"It doesn't look like I'm going to have permission to go in and get Stephens until he kills someone," I said.

"So what are they letting us do?" Wayne asked. "Set up an ambush?"

I nodded. "I don't know for sure that he'll come out of the hills on Thursday or Friday, but that's pretty much his MO. When he does come down, it's anywhere from late morning to early evening. That's a lot of hours lying out in the desert sun."

"A lot of hours," Wayne said.

"I need someone I can count on. I need someone who knows

what Stephens is really about. You're the man. So what do you think? You up for a couple of days in the desert?"

"Let's do it."

"We're going to need rifles and plenty of water, my friend. I'll pick up everything we need. We'll set up an ambush. If Stephens wants to take us on, we'll take him out."

Wayne would need to get the okay from his group supervisor, which wouldn't be a problem. Everybody in the division had confidence in Wayne Morrison. Besides, we had Skopeck's blessing to set up on the trail.

Thursday morning came, and I drove to Wayne's house to pick him up. I'd dressed in cammies and had provisions. I figured that an AR-15 with a couple of thirty-round magazines and a six-shot revolver would be sufficient for the operation. Wayne was dressed in camouflage and packing his own AR and a revolver. We headed out for breakfast to finalize the plan. As we ate, we ran through a number of possible scenarios, but it all came down to one thing: We weren't taking any chances with this guy, whatever happened.

At nine A.M. we headed toward Rancho Cucamonga. We found a place to stash my G-ride and began humping up the wash, looking for a good place to set up on Stephens's trail. About halfway up the hill to the wash area, we came upon a berm that was about ten or fifteen feet high, with the trail cutting a cap through it. It was a perfect place to set up an ambush. Wayne took a position on one side of the trail concealed by the berm, and I did the same on the other side.

We decided that when Stephens approached, I would draw

his attention, and if he made a move, Wayne would have a clear shot from his flank. It was pretty simple. We settled in as the sun made its way to the center of the sky. Ten turned to twelve to two to four, with no sight of movement on the trail. Just the unforgiving desert sun. As the sun started to set to the west, I heard myself grumbling. "What a fucking waste of time this turned out to be . . ."

We made our way back to the car around six that evening. I told Wayne I would have to come back and try tomorrow. Wayne didn't hesitate in agreeing.

"I'll pick you up first thing in the morning," I said. "Should be another day of tarantula watching."

We convinced ourselves that we'd have a somewhat better chance of catching Stephens on a Friday.

Friday morning I picked up Wayne, and again we headed to the stash area in Rancho Cucamonga to hide the G-ride. Even more intent on taking Stephens down today, I had packed another thirty-round magazine; something in my gut had told me to bring extra ammo.

We made our way to the ambush site and settled in with more confidence. Our tension heightened as every hour went by. I peeked over the berm every few minutes in anticipation of the confrontation. Twelve rolled by. It got mighty hot.

Wayne and I talked about what would happen if we had to shoot Stephens. We talked about what would happen if we had to shoot Skopeck.

We talked about how big the fallout would be if we threw out the rule book and went up into the hills after Stephens. We talked and talked until six o'clock rolled around.

I was pissed. If we'd humped it up that mountain, we could have been sitting in Stephens's camp with all his grass stuffed up his ass.

"Sorry, Wayne," I said. "Let's get the fuck out of here."

As we started our trek back to the car, the thought occurred to me that Stephens might have known we were down there all along and had been sitting out of range, waiting for us to make a move.

I didn't know what to make of it. Why hadn't he come down from the hills? Had someone gotten the word to him?

Whatever the reason, we were coming away empty-handed. I wanted to blame someone: Skopeck, Pratt, Stephens, it didn't matter. Our failure made me angrier and my resolve stronger. I looked at Wayne as we threw our AR-15s in the car.

"I'm gonna get him, Wayne, no matter what. I'm gonna fuckin' get him."

Wayne nodded. "We'll get him, Bill."

Twelve

Beyond the obstacle of not having the official green light to go up into the hills to get Stephens, I had an even bigger problem. I had a vague idea but no real specifics about where his camp actually was, even though I had been to the wash in Rancho Cucamonga so many times, staring up at the mountains, hoping for some evidence of the camp's location.

I knew that the San Bernardino SWAT boys had gotten a look at Stephens's camp and his marijuana fields. They were my best source for locating the camp.

I still had little reconnaissance intel for what I was dealing with when it came to terrain and vegetation in those mountains near the Cajon Pass. One thing I was certain of was the potential for a bad spontaneous brush fire. I had seen plenty of fires around the L.A. area, and there was plenty of fuel in the hills above the Cajon Pass.

As I cruised east on the 10 freeway, the Santa Ana winds were blasting down from the Cajon Pass. Those famous hot winds are their strongest in this area and are so fierce that they can lay semi trucks and RV campers on their sides. At times those giant vehicles litter the highways like dead dinosaurs. Stick a match to the fuel in the hills, add a Santa Ana wind, and you've got a formula that makes national news.

I rolled into the Berdoo Sheriff's Department and lucked out, running into Captain Mike Cardwell, who had been with the department for a long time. He was a real go-getter and was in charge of their SWAT team.

"Just the man I was looking for," I said. "I need to talk with you about our mutual friend Mark Stephens."

I told him I thought everybody had had just about enough of that guy, and I wanted to put together an operation to go in and get him.

"'Bout time, too," he said. "I figured ATF or one of the fed agencies would sooner or later end up in the chase."

Cardwell told me that he had done several operations with ATF and that Berdoo liked working with us. He repeated what I'd been saying: It was only a matter of time before Stephens killed someone with that MAC-10. The Rancho Cucamonga office had contacted him a number of times, wanting Berdoo SWAT to take this guy out. He was glad that ATF had decided at long last to go get him.

"Well," I admitted, "we've still got to get the all-clear from the brass."

"Look, Queen," he said, "I was there myself. I was up in the hills, watching this idiot humping water and tending his pot patches. It gave us all chills to see him moving around with that MAC-10 hanging around his neck. Especially knowin' that he's the kind of dude who's got no qualms whatsoever about using it."

Cardwell said that Berdoo SWAT would support any operation ATF wanted. But he stressed that attempting to go into the mountains after Stephens would be a risky operation. He told me they'd made several air recon missions into the hills, which I had already heard about, and that even spotting Stephens's camp from the air was a challenge.

"He's no fool, this guy. He knows a thing or two about camouflage," he said.

"That's all right," I said. "So do I."

I was glad to hear about Berdoo's enthusiasm. I was also glad to know that someone besides Bill Kendrick and I knew how dangerous Stephens was. Cardwell said to let him know if I wanted to do a recon mission. Tom Federoff in the Berdoo air unit knew just about where Stephens's camp was, and he would be glad to set that up.

Under a week later, I made a trip out to the Berdoo air facility in Rialto to hook up with Tom Federoff. When I got there, a sheriff's deputy told me that Federoff was on his way in with his chopper to meet me. We were standing outside when Federoff made his appearance in an old slick overhead.

Instead of landing right away, Federoff maneuvered his chopper to a rappel tower that had a railing around the top. He balanced the skids on the rail for maybe thirty seconds. As we stood there watching this display of chopper talent, I knew I wanted him flying for us. "Holy shit," I said. "This guy is no joke."

Tom Federoff was a Vietnam-vet chopper pilot looking for a challenge. I wondered aloud if we could get him to do a flyby and send a few rockets whizzing into Stephens's camp.

Federoff set the chopper down and exited. Watching him took me back to my tour of duty in the Special Forces. In his chopper helmet, he even looked like an old-time 'Nam pilot.

"That was some impressive flying, Mr. Federoff," I said, extending my hand and introducing myself.

"Greetings, Bill Queen," Federoff said. "I heard you got some work for us."

"Sure as hell do. You know a thing or two about this Mark Stephens?"

"Yup. Been over his camp a few times," Federoff said.

"Let's go get him," I said.

Federoff laughed. "Sure thing."

"I need to do a recon mission up there and get you guys to point out where you think his camp is."

Without hesitation, Federoff said, "Hell, let's do it now."

He and his spotter turned and headed back to the chopper. I retrieved my camera from my Mustang and ran back to the chopper. Federoff was throwing switches and firing up the helicopter. His spotter handed me a set of headphones, and I slipped them on.

"Hook up your seat belt, Bill!"

I had ridden with several cowboys in Vietnam who had scared the shit out of me, and I couldn't help but flash back to a couple of those white-knuckle rides. There was no M60 hanging out the door, and I didn't have to worry about Vietcong taking potshots at us. But it sure felt quite a bit like 'Nam.

Federoff wound up the rotor, barely cleared the ground, then dumped the nose. He was definitely a throwback 'Nam pilot, even if this was twenty years later and half a world away. He turned the chopper and headed north, climbing as fast and as high as the old slick would allow. It was only seconds before we got a crystal-clear view of the San Bernardino Mountains, with Stephens's refuge somewhere in that massive wilderness.

"Okay, Bill. We're going to do an east-to-west pass first. I'll let you know when we're getting close, and the spotter will point out the area."

Federoff tucked the chopper in close to the mountain. "We don't need to do this but a couple of times. We don't want to alert Stephens that we're on to him."

I nodded. "You're right. I don't want to do that."

I kept leaning out the door, looking for the bad guys, just as I had done in 1970. The mission this time would be different, if no less dangerous.

The spotter keyed the mike. "Okay, Bill, see the trail leading up the mountain into the brush? If you drop down into the gulley and work your way up the mountain, Stephens's camp is about three quarters of the way up the mountain. It's hard to spot. As a matter of fact, we've never actually seen the camp from the air, only his marijuana fields."

I squinted but couldn't see anything discernible.

"There!" he said. "Just up the gulley side. The east side. You can see one of his fields. Did you see it?"

I strained to search the area, but I didn't see it. "Shit, I missed it," I said.

"That's okay," Federoff said. "We'll make another pass."

We flew farther west until we were out of the area, then turned and tucked in against the mountain again. This pass I was sitting on Federoff's side of the chopper.

"Bill," the spotter said, "look down at the gulley until you see what looks to be a serious rock cliff. Look up the hill a bit more and to the east. You'll see a small patch that looks like a light greenish area. That's a marijuana patch. See it?"

I strained again. "Oh, yeah," I said finally. "I do see it."

I wasn't much of a marijuana-patch spotter; I'd never had much training in that skill. There are cops who do grass spotting all the time during growing season. They get so good they can spot the weed fields during nighttime recon flights.

Though I saw the light green patch, I still wasn't sure what I was looking at. At least now I had a pretty good idea where the camp was. But I was so busy trying to spot something that I didn't take any pictures, and I didn't want to risk another flyby, at least not today. Too much helicopter beating overhead, and who knew what Stephens would do?

We headed back to Rialto. To my surprise, Federoff did another rail stand before we landed. He was a daredevil, all right. I guess it was some type of welcome-home exercise for him. He had it down pat.

After landing, Federoff and I went to the hangar and talked about Stephens and the possible operation into the hills.

"Look, Bill," he said, "I'll back you to the edge of the envelope. But let me tell you first about the envelope. Heat and altitude are killers for helicopter operations. Stephens is far enough up the hill that it could be a problem if the sun gets hot."

I knew this information full well from my past work with helicopters and airplanes; at higher altitudes, the air gets thinner, of course, making it more difficult to maintain your aircraft's elevation. The intense California heat, would only compound the problem of staying up.

"Another thing," Federoff continued. "Flying around mountains at night is always dangerous. You can't see the hills properly. I may be a cowboy, but I'm not that much of a cowboy. So flying into the mountains at night is out. Last and definitely not least: There is virtually no place to set a chopper down up there. You need to figure that into your ops plan."

I took note of Federoff's concerns.

"But besides that," he said, "everything else is in bounds. If your boy Stephens starts shooting, I'll carry a gunslinger or two on board to back your play."

Federoff was dead serious, and I knew it. When I left, I had a good feeling about my air support, if I could get the operation green-lit.

I would need to get back in the air and take some photos of the area. But I didn't want to exhaust Tom Federoff's generosity. Next time I would hook up with our own air support guy, a great pilot and friend of mine named Jay Lanning.

I called Jay and set up a recon mission. I told him that my most pressing problem was learning the precise coordinates of Stephens's camp; I didn't want to make the same mistakes that the Fontana and Berdoo SWAT teams had made. Jay was a full-time pilot for ATF who'd flown several missions for me in the past. He said no problem, we would buzz the mountains, and I'd get some aerial photographs, hopefully even a picture of Stephens's camp.

But that was easier said than done. I would soon learn exactly why Fontana and Berdoo had been forced to cut their SWAT missions short.

Jay Lanning flew out of the Riverside airport and piloted a Partenavia, a twin-engine, high-wing spotter-type aircraft. Unlike Tom Federoff, he had learned to fly with ATF and was a fixed-wing pilot. Jay wasn't into the cowboy stuff like Federoff, but he did love to fly.

Later that week, we hooked up in the early morning, and he showed me his plane. The Partenavia is an Italian-made aircraft known for being especially good at high-altitude spotting and surveillance. I told Jay I had been at the base of the mountains on numerous occasions and even on Stephens's trail a couple of times.

Jay fired up the airplane, and we took to the sky. It was only a few minutes until we were over the Berdoo Mountains— climbing to the necessary altitude took longer than actually getting to the hills. I vectored Jay into the area, and this time I had my camera ready. I started clicking off the pictures as soon as we got close. We made a pass by the area where I believed Stephens's camp was, though I still couldn't spot it.

In addition to being an excellent pilot, Jay was a good spotter. But he couldn't spot the camp, either. Jay turned the airplane around to make another pass, this time a little closer down toward the mountain.

I could see the rough red granite of the range below. The mountains were a lot rougher than I had imagined: The gullies were deeper, and the vegetation was denser than it seemed from down in the valley. I readied my camera, but again, neither Jay nor I could spot the camp with the naked eye.

Marijuana plants are a different color than the indigenous plants in the mountains of California, but even concentrating on those light green patches, we couldn't seem to spot the camp. Again, I didn't want to make too many passes for fear of alerting Stephens. I told Jay to make a final flyover, and I'd snap as many pictures as I could of the area, then we'd get the hell out of there.

My thinking was, if I snapped enough pictures we could blow them up in the lab and surely get one or two images of the camp. I could sit down with Steve Kilgore, with the Berdoo and Fontana SWAT guys, and have them pinpoint where they thought the camp was.

I wanted to recon the trail. I wanted to know where Stephens had put his booby traps. It was crucial information to have if I was ever going to put together an ops plan. I wanted Stephens bad, but not at the cost of getting anyone hurt.

We landed back at Riverside, and I hit the highway with my newly acquired intelligence photos. After getting the film developed, I was sorely disappointed. In all those dozens of photographs, I had only one showing a field of marijuana. None of our experts could actually see the camp—such were Stephens's skills at camouflaging his hideout to blend in with the natural terrain.

But I knew one thing. The camp couldn't be too far from that marijuana field. It wasn't the best intel, but it looked like the best we could do.

Thirteen

t had been almost two weeks since Wayne Morrison and I
had set up on Stephens's trail over the Cajon Pass. We tried
a couple more times but couldn't wait in the desert heat
indefinitely. And sure enough, when we weren't there lying in
ambush, Mark Stephens made another trip down from his
mountain hideout.

This time he needed to get some medical attention. He had
gotten into it with a badger in the mountains that acted like it
had more right to the camp than Stephens did; Stephens was
pretty lucky that he came out on top. Once he was fixed up, he
went to visit one of his regular dealers operated in the city of
Upland, an upscale community nestled next to the mountains

just inside the county of San Bernardino. His Upland connection, a young guy named Gary, wasn't a real hard-core criminal. Gary dealt small-time grass and wasn't known to be particularly violent, so he wasn't much of a concern to local law enforcement.

Stephens pulled up in front of Gary's house in the early afternoon. Gary was just a middleman, and his network of street dealers hadn't yet paid him for the grass he'd fronted them. Fronting dope to a dealer is kind of like dropping money into a slot machine in Vegas. Doesn't often pay off.

Stephens told Gary that he'd stopped by to pick up his money. Gary got nervous and started to hem and haw. Then he told Stephens the truth: He didn't have it. As soon as Stephens learned that he would be walking away empty-handed, he made it clear that Gary wouldn't be walking away at all.

Gary was scared shitless. He was all too aware of Stephens's violent nature, and more than once he'd seen the bloody results firsthand. He assured Stephens that he could go get the money from one of his street dealers, a kid named Sonny, who owed him.

Stephens looked at Gary for a long moment, gripping his .45. "Okay," he said. "Let's go get it from him."

All Gary wanted was to get away from Stephens with his life.

"Let's go!" Stephens yelled. They loaded up in Gary's car and headed for Sonny's house. Sonny also lived in the Upland area. It didn't take much time to find out that he wasn't at home. But Stephens didn't care; it wasn't Sonny who owed him the money, it was Gary.

Gary could feel the tension building in the car. Stephens was starting to shake, and his eyes were staring in a frighteningly blank way. Gary was talking for all his life was worth, hoping Stephens wouldn't suddenly snap.

Stephens had his gun resting on his thigh. His finger was on the trigger. Gary was jabbering about borrowing the money, selling his car, doing whatever he had to do to get Stephens his dough, when right there in front of the car they spotted Sonny walking down the sidewalk.

Gary sighed with relief. He turned to Stephens and said that he was about to get his money. Gary pulled his car to the side of the road and hollered to Sonny. Gary and Sonny had been friends since they were little kids, but right now, as far as Gary was concerned, it was all business.

"Just hang here a minute," Gary said to Stephens, getting out of the car.

"What's up?" Sonny said, approaching them.

"Man," Gary said, "am I glad to see you. I need to get that money for the grass I fronted you."

"I ain't got it on me," Sonny said. "I'll have it for you in a few days."

"Shit, I need it fuckin' right now."

"I don't have it right now."

"Well, you need to get it right now!"

"Gary," Sonny said, "I can't. I'm short. I told you, it'll take me a few days to get it, okay? Is that so fuckin' hard to under-stand?"

Friendship or not, Gary was in a panic and looking for a

scapegoat. He glanced back to the car, at the waiting gun-toting maniac in the passenger seat.

"You fucking idiot!" Gary said. "I need my money right now!"

Sonny had never seen Gary so belligerent. "Tough luck, pal," he said. "I don't have the money right now, so you'll have to wait till I get it."

Gary knew it was his ass on the line. He snapped and sucker punched Sonny square in the face.

Sonny was no shrinking violet. He staggered back with his nose bloodied, then he came back with a combination of his own. The fight was on. After exchanging a couple more haymakers to the gut, the two men tangled up in a clinch and rolled to the sidewalk.

They were fighting right in the heart of downtown Upland, only a block from the Upland Police Department.

After a minute of watching them grappling and slugging, Mark Stephens had had enough. He didn't give a shit about the fight, but he was pissed that he wouldn't be getting his money. He hopped out of the car and walked over to where they were sprawled on the sidewalk, choking and punching each other.

Stephens raised his .45 and fired one round into Sonny's leg.

All the fight drained out of Sonny. Gary stood up, stunned, waiting for Stephens to put a bullet into him, too.

Stephens stood over Sonny. "I oughta finish off the fucker," he said calmly.

"Jesus Christ, Mark, no," Gary said. "Let's get the fuck out of here before the cops get here."

Stephens snapped back to consciousness. "Yeah, let's get the fuck out of here."

For all his psychotic rage, Stephens had enough sense to know that every time he assaulted, pistol-whipped, or shot someone, he had to get out of town. There were witnesses up and down the block who'd seen him shoot Sonny in the leg. As bad as he wanted his money, it wasn't worth going to jail over. And as much as he wanted to shoot Gary in the face, he must've known that wouldn't be too cool—not in broad daylight and in front of a half-dozen witnesses. Plus, he did need Gary's help to make his escape back to the hills.

Stephens's eyes darted up and down the block. He tucked his gun away. "Take me over to my parents' house," he said, jumping in the car.

Gary was hardly in a position to argue; he raced back toward Rancho Cucamonga. As they got farther away from the scene, the quiet, trancelike rage started to set in. Stephens kept repeating the same words, saying that this was all Gary's fault, and if anything happened because of it, he was holding Gary responsible. As they pulled up to Valley Street, Stephens turned and stared at Gary. "You better get my money and fuckin' quick," he said. "The next time I see you, if you don't have the money, I'm gonna blow your brains out."

Stephens had to lam it out of town; he would need to let the heat die down before he could be seen traveling around the Inland Empire. He'd be ducking and dodging the cops this time and would have to stay off the main streets and keep an eye out. If anyone got in his way, it would be bad news.

had just left the San Bernardino Sheriff's Department when I got a page from Kevin. I initially thought I'd wait until I got back into the Ontario area before I called him. But something told me Kevin might have a real-time fix on Stephens.

I got off the 10 freeway in Fontana and hit the nearest pay phone. "Yo, Kevin, what's up?"

Sure enough, Kevin had information on Stephens.

Stephens had been seen in Rancho Cucamonga near his parents' house not over twenty minutes earlier. Kevin said that Stephens was on his way back to the mountains and that he'd probably stop to pick up provisions at the little convenience store he often frequented.

"Thanks, Kevin," I said, and ran back to my Mustang. I revved it up and got on the radio. I needed somebody to head for Rancho Cucamonga to try and set up a trap for Stephens, but I couldn't reach Wayne Morrison, so I called the Metro office and had them give the Berdoo Sheriff's Department a call.

I gunned my souped-up G-ride on the 10 freeway. I must have been running over a hundred miles an hour, flicking the radio on and off, swerving through the slower traffic, and I didn't notice the California Highway Patrol lighting me up until I heard the siren. I knew that trying to throw up my own red light now would be pointless.

I pulled the Mustang onto the shoulder. I saw the approaching CHP officer in my rearview and could tell he was pissed. The patrolman pulled his gun and pointed it at me as he approached my car. I already had my ATF badge out and was loudly shouting out the open window: "Federal agent! Federal agent!"

Didn't calm the guy down much. He was bright red in the face. "Just where the hell are you going?"

"I'm on official business, and I'm in a hurry."

"Yeah, I can see that."

I slipped my badge out the window to him.

"You got some ID to go with that badge?" he said.

"Sure," I said, and flipped my creds out.

He took them and gave me a once-over, frowning with contempt, before handing them back. "You need to slow it down, Mr. Fed." He turned and walked back to his patrol car.

Slow it down? I hit the gas hard and headed for Cucamonga. The radio clicked in again. Division had gotten in touch with the Berdoo sheriff's department, and they had a car headed for Stephens's parents' house. They'd surely get there before me, I thought. I hoped the deputy knew what he was getting himself into.

My tires shrieked as I headed north in Rancho Cucamonga. I was worried about the Berdoo sheriff's deputy who had been sent to Stephens's parents' place. Would he understand that Stephens wouldn't hesitate to open fire on a lawman?

I pushed the car harder and drove right within sight of a Berdoo motorcycle cop running a radar gun. I knew he had me the minute I spotted him, and I pulled over as quickly as I could. "Jesus," I said, "are you fuckin' kidding me?"

The cop sat on his bike running my tag and didn't approach the car. I got out, and he shouted angrily, ordering me back in the car. I held up my badge and yelled back at him. "I'm a fed! I'm on my way to back up one of your units!"

He got off his bike and approached me. "What's that?"

"I'm on my way to back up a Berdoo sheriff's unit. I'm meeting up with your own guys," I said.

I flipped my creds over for him to see. He took a quick look and waved me on. I ran back to the car, jumped in, hit the gas, and headed for Stephens's parents' place. As I turned onto Valley Street, I could see the Berdoo sheriff's car sitting a couple of blocks down from the house. I pulled up behind the sheriff's car and got out; the deputy got out of his vehicle, too. He already knew who I was. "Looking for Stephens, huh?" he said. He told me he hadn't seen Stephens or any movement to or from his parents' place.

The deputy had received word that I'd been stopped by a traffic unit on the way there.

"That's only half of it," I said, laughing. "I got stopped on the 10 by a Chippy before that."

The deputy said he'd been chasing Stephens himself. He knew that Stephens had been hiding in the hills for several years and that he was one armed and dangerous psycho. The deputy knew of two shootings in the area in which Mark Stephens was the prime suspect, and he said that he thought Stephens was good for a couple of other shootings in his jurisdiction as well, but no one could prove it.

I felt better knowing that everybody in area law enforcement knew about Mark Stephens and just how dangerous he was. I was worried that Stephens might have lost it today and decided to gun down his own parents, but I didn't vocalize my fears. I told the deputy to sit tight on his surveillance, and I'd head up to the convenience store where I knew Stephens bought his provisions. We said we'd maintain radio contact.

On the way, I thought it would be better to head toward the wash leading to the mountains and work my way back down to the store. I pulled my 9mm from its holster and laid it on the seat beside me. As I pulled up to the wash, my heart slid into my gut.

I saw a figure quickly walking north on the access road that ran next to the wash. White male, late thirties, unkempt appearance. Had to be Stephens.

I'd have to go into overdrive to catch up with him. If I turned onto the access road and he saw me, he'd run into the brush, and I'd never flush him out. He'd also know that his hideout in the hills had been compromised. Who knew what irrational course of action he'd take next?

I pulled my car to the side of the road and got my AR-15 out of the trunk. Staying low and off the road, I headed through the brush on foot. I wasn't dressed for the chase. Wearing a pair of new loafers, and humping a radio in one hand and an AR-15 in the other, I'd jogged about a quarter mile when I started feeling nauseated. It must have been a combination of nerves and not being prepared for running at a good clip.

I could see Stephens better, and I knew that if I could only keep going I would soon overtake him. But I didn't have much time. Stephens would be off the access road in a minute and then up the hills and into the brush. I had no hope of following him into the wilderness.

I pushed myself harder, sprinting, gasping to the point where I had to stop. I was huffing and puffing, my hands on my knees. I couldn't control it. First I dry-heaved, and then I puked. With my hands still on my knees, I could see Stephens climbing the first hill at the end of the wash.

I could see him clearly now, and he could have obviously seen me if he'd turned around. I ducked down behind a scrub bush, furious that Stephens was slipping away from me. My rifle had a scope on it; I leveled it at Stephens and watched through it as he climbed into the hills. With my crosshairs centered on Stephens, I thought about the terror he had brought to the people in the valley. If I didn't stop him now, he was going to kill someone. I actually started to move the safety switch to fire, but then I came to my senses. I was a lawman, not an assassin. I had to bring Stephens back alive.

I collapsed to the ground and lay there till the sickness started to subside. My radio started to crackle.

"One-four," came the call from Berdoo. "One-one."

"One-one," I tried to respond. "Go, One-one."

Again came the call: "One-four, One-one . . ."

Again I tried to respond: "Go ahead, One-one!"

Several more times One-one tried to make contact, but they couldn't hear my reply. I could make sense of their transmission. The Berdoo sheriff had found my abandoned Mustang and had contacted division to see if anyone had radio contact with me. One-one and the Berdoo sheriff had each sent a couple of black-and-whites my way. I could hear the traffic but was unable to make myself heard on my radio.

I knew that if they considered me an officer in distress, it would be a matter of minutes before police cars would be everywhere. I began jogging back down the hill as best I could. I ran over the jagged rocks, chewing up my loafers. I wanted to get back on the access road, but I knew Stephens could see me there. He would have a clear shot at me if he decided to take it. I also knew Stephens would see all the police cars at the wash if I couldn't make it back in time, so I sped up even more. It took a good five minutes to make it back to the street, running as hard as I could. The Berdoo deputy saw me and pulled his car onto the access road. I waved my hands, signaling him to back up. He didn't get the message. Huffing and puffing, I ran up next to his car and told him to pull back onto the street and drive down to where my car was.

I ran back to my car and got on the radio, trying desperately to avert the shit storm of wailing patrol cars.

"One-one, One-four!" I shouted.

One-one responded instantly. "One-four, go ahead."

"Yeah, One-one. I was caught out of radio range. You can call off the backup units. Call 'em all off."

One-one responded: "One-four, get to a land line and 10-21 the office."

10-21 is cop-speak for making a telephone call. I knew that 10-21 to the Metro office meant I'd have to tell Chuck Pratt how close I'd come to nabbing Stephens down from the mountain. I wasn't looking forward to telling him that Stephens had gotten away again.

Fourteen

By the early summer of '86, Mark Stephens had shot up several locations in the Inland Empire. He had brazenly shot and nearly killed Sonny just one block from the Upland Police Department. He had assaulted several others and left no mistake in anyone's mind that he was prepared to kill. The final straw for me was getting word that Stephens had been down in Montclair again; this time he had stuck a gun in a girl's mouth and nearly scared her to death.

Stephens was looking for one of his dealers, and he went to the dealer's sister's house looking for him. The dealer wasn't there, but the sister was. Stephens was livid. He grabbed the sister and literally shoved his gun in her mouth, yelling, "If you don't tell me where your brother is, I'm going to blow your fucking brains out." She was petrified. She didn't know where her brother was, so she believed she was dead for sure. But apparently Stephens thought better of killing her and let her go.

People were going to die soon. I wasn't the only one to see it. Now Chuck Pratt was all for going into the hills to get Stephens. He had made formal appeals to Robert Skopeck several times, to no avail.

I was at the end of my rope. I had played the cat-and-mouse game with Stephens long enough. There were plenty of state warrants for his arrest, but they weren't carrying much weight around the division office. I went to the federal courthouse downtown, put in the requisite hours getting the legal work done, and left the courthouse with a federal warrant for Mark Stephens's arrest, on multiple counts of violating Title 26 Section 5861(d), possession of Title III weapons (machine guns and hand grenades).

I walked over to the division office and knocked fiercely on Robert Skopeck's door. His secretary looked at me as if I either had a death wish or didn't mind being transferred to Pigslop, Oklahoma, for the rest of my ATF days. Not waiting for an invitation, I opened the door and walked right up to Skopeck's desk.

"With all due respect, sir," I said, "I've tried for weeks now to do things your way. To catch Stephens the way you wanted me to. Every week that goes by, he shoots up another place or terrorizes another community. The locals need ATF leadership on this. Stephens is in possession of machine guns and hand grenades and is growing marijuana openly on federal land. If we keep going with this cat-and-mouse game, I have no doubt that I'm soon going to be right back here, standing in front of this desk, telling you that Stephens killed someone."

"What are you proposing, Agent?" Skopeck said. He was glaring, but I wasn't sure if he was pissed or skeptical.

"What I've been saying all along, sir. We've got no other options. We've got to go into the mountains and get him ourselves."

Skopeck looked at me hard for a couple of seconds. I braced myself for the worst.

"Have you exhausted every other means to catch him?"

"Yessir, I have."

"All right, Agent Queen," Skopeck said. "Go on back to your office, and I'll let your group supervisor know when I've made a decision."

Somehow I'd made it this far without being verbally abused or put on notice regarding my transfer. I decided not to push my luck. I left Skopeck's office without feeling like I had won or lost, but I had made a point. I'd gone on record. If something bad did happen, Skopeck would have it sitting on his shoulders.

The operation I was asking for was an enormous risk. I left it to Skopeck to decide which was more appealing: having to explain a shoot-out or maybe even an agent getting killed in the line of duty, or having to explain why he'd let a violent drug trafficker continue to operate until he committed premeditated murder, after being warned numerous times about the threat risk.

I knew that the SAC would be thinking about the political fallout of his decision. I also knew that I'd jumped the chain of command, and that meant my immediate superior, Chuck Pratt, could be the target of Skopeck's rage. Bosses really hate that jumping-chain-of-command bullshit. But I was beyond caring about the politics. They seemed a bit petty compared to what was happening out in the Inland Empire.

It was toward the end of the day when Chuck Pratt called me. "Queen, I want to see you in my office!"

God, I hated the sound of those words. It usually meant something other than an "Attaboy, Billy."

I walked in and sat down in front of Pratt's American and Marine Corps flags. Chuck glared at me like he wanted to punch my lights out. Before he could give me the news, I spoke up. "Did I get you in trouble?" I knew Pratt had gotten a ream job from Skopeck. The look on his face confirmed it.

But Pratt was a tough old marine and pretty good at fading the heat. He dodged my question completely. "All right, Queen, get your ops plan together," he said. "We're going into the mountains."

I was stunned. I wanted to say, "About fuckin' time!," but I held back. "We're really doing this, Chuck?"

"It came straight from Skopeck. Go ahead and pick your team."

The decision took a minute to sink in. My emotions were jumping all over the map. I was relieved on one hand, but I was

ARMED and DANGEROUS

also nervous, because I knew the mission was going to be dangerous, and I didn't want to be responsible for getting anybody hurt or killed. I could do the mission myself; I had no doubt about that. But if I humped up the mountain on my own, I knew I'd end up in a gunfight with Stephens.

"You got it, Chuck," I said. "I'll start picking the team."

Pratt said I could pick whomever I wanted, but he made it clear that he would be one of the members of the team. I didn't have a problem with that.

When I got up to leave the room, I felt elated. The bickering and consulting were finally over. It wasn't a question of whether we were going to take Stephens down. Now it was a matter of logistics.

I had a lot of work to do before we actually put a foot on the ground. As much as I hated sitting down and doing the paper, it didn't seem so bad now. I had the warrant I needed. Stephens was on federal land, and I had the backing from ATF. Stephens was on his way down.

I went back to my desk and began to imagine how this operation was going to play out. As far as who was going in with me, I knew I wanted only one person by my side: Wayne Morrison. I knew that Wayne and I, with our Special Forces training, could do the operation by ourselves. We didn't need anyone else. But Chuck Pratt and Robert Skopeck would never go for that.

On the upside, because the division office knew this would be a dangerous mission, I wouldn't have a problem getting anyone I wanted in the entire division. I had run this scenario through

167

my head countless times, back when it was wishful thinking. We had some good agents in the office. Ken Cates had a ton of heart and was the kind of guy who'd walk through hell for his brother agents. Chuck Pratt and Lanny Royer also had heart. I didn't know Steve Kilgore too well, but he was enthusiastic, and he knew the area where Stephens's camp was. Howard Sanders was a good friend and would do almost anything I wanted him to do.

One by one, I reached out for my team members.

I got Wayne Morrison on the line first. "Wayne, guess what? We're going in the hills for Stephens."

Wayne was calm, as always. "I'm ready," he said. "Just let me know when."

It was Friday morning, so I told Wayne that we'd have to wait until Tuesday or Wednesday. He agreed that midweek we would be most likely to catch Stephens in his camp, and he said he'd let his Arson Group supervisor know.

Next I called up Steve Kilgore. Steve and I had talked about the communications problems in the mountains, and I told him that the radio system he used in the U.S. Forest Service would probably function better than ATF's. Steve said that we could count on him for the radios and that he'd be there for the briefing in my office on Monday. He would bring the Forest Service radios so the team could be briefed on their operation.

I then walked across the office to Ken Cates's desk and told him I wanted him to be on the team. Ken assured me he would be there. I found Howard Sanders and told him that the operation was on for next Tuesday and Wednesday. Howard looked at me with a little concern. "Okay, Billy," he said. "Just let me know what you need." Howard isn't much of a woodsman. The zoo is about as close to wildlife as he wants to get.

"Thanks."

The guys all seemed psyched that the operation was finally coming together.

I went back to my desk and started putting together an operational plan. I had played the takedown of Stephens over and over in my head. I had to get serious and put it down on paper so it would be acceptable to the brass.

We'd use a seven-man team. Wayne Morrison and I would be a two-man recon squad. We would slip in before dawn, under the cover of darkness, and put eyes on the camp before the arrest-and-extraction team moved in. Arrest-and-extraction would consist of Ken Cates, Lanny Royer, Steve Kilgore, and Chuck Pratt. Base-camp security and communications relay would be held by Howard Sanders.

This operation would be a bit unusual for ATF in that it would be more like a military raid than our standard residential door-kicking takedowns. We would be moving like a crack military special-ops unit, ascending through the hills in stealth, on the lookout for booby traps and early-warning devices. As I typed up the paperwork, I tried not to overemphasize the military-type operational side for fear of giving the brass second thoughts. We wouldn't be needing armored vehicles or electronic surveillance equipment, and we didn't need to draw ATF money for the operation. It was pretty much straight up, as far as the brass needed to know.

I began to list the equipment I needed. Hand grenades were out. Fire support was out. We'd be armed with AR-15s and sidearms.

I called Berdoo SWAT and told Mike Cardwell that we were green-lit to go into the hills for Stephens. I requested backup from his team, and without hesitation, he said he would notify his people. He'd plan for his boys to spend the night at the air support facility on Tuesday night and to be there until we were safely down from the hills. Mike said he would make all the arrangements, and I was grateful. He was a true professional who took his job seriously. He had already been involved with one failed attempt to apprehend Stephens, and I didn't need to convince him of this operation's potential to go bad.

As I left for home, I made a note to spend at least part of the weekend mounting a scope on my AR and zeroing it in. I was excited and nervous at the same time. I was going to confront the infamous Mark Stephens at last, though it wasn't going to be easy. I'd never had a problem confronting dangerous situations, but this time I was taking friends with me. True, they were law enforcement agents, like me, but they were also friends, and I didn't like putting my friends in harm's way.

Lanny Royer was one of my best friends in ATF; our wives and families even socialized on the weekends. Lanny hadn't been in the office when I'd gotten the word from Pratt, so I called him at home that evening. Judy, Lanny's wife, answered the phone, and we exchanged pleasantries before I told her I needed to catch up with Lanny real quick.

"Sure, Bill, hold on."

I thought about Judy and their three kids. *Jesus,* I thought. *What am I getting everybody into?*

Lanny got on the phone. "What's up, dude?"

"Lanny, you know that fuckin' bad actor Mark Stephens I've been chasing for the past couple of months?"

"Sure. What about him?"

"I just got the word from on high. We're going into the mountains to take him out. You up for it?"

Lanny didn't hesitate. "Hell, yeah. Count me in."

"Next Tuesday and Wednesday I'll need you."

"Two days?"

"Yup. Just think of it as kind of an ATF-sponsored camping trip."

Lanny laughed.

"I'm putting things together this weekend. We'll have a briefing on Monday. Can you handle all that?"

"I'll be there, buddy. No problem."

When I hung up, I realized how tough it would be to separate my concern for my friends from the necessary operational procedures. In the military, they have a phrase: "acceptable losses." On this operation, there would be no acceptable losses—not for ATF, and especially not for me.

To minimize the risk to the team overall, I planned for Wayne Morrison and me to shoulder the bulk of the danger. I ran scenario after scenario through my head. It would have to be Wayne and me who took Stephens off. The rest of the team was rock-solid—I knew that—but I had the ultimate faith in Wayne and me. We were both former SF. We'd chewed some of the same dirt in 'Nam. I knew I could trust him with my life, and the feeling was mutual.

Fifteen

Saturday morning I woke up and drove to the firing range in Chino to get my AR-15 scope zeroed in. If I had my way, we'd all be going in "heavy"—Wayne and I carrying hand grenades and machine guns. I would have at least one sniper, and our air support could lay down some heavy cover.

It wasn't our mission to get anybody killed, at least none of the good guys. Stephens wasn't going to play by any rules. Why should we? That was the hand I was dealt, though. Cops often have the cards stacked against them, at least in terms of firepower and reckless abandon—that's why we have to train to be so much better than the bad guys.

Mark Stephens presented a formidable opponent. He was

mean, aggressive, and well armed. He had the home-court advantage, and he wasn't bound by any conduct of ethics. It didn't seem fair to me. I wondered if I should throw the ATF rule book out the window and convert my AR-15 to full auto—there were certainly enough full-auto conversion parts lying around in the Metro Group office. But if I went fully automatic and there was a shoot-out, there'd be hell to pay with the adminners.

No, I'd have to settle for my AR with a scope. If it came down to a long-distance shoot-out, I'd have the advantage, even if Stephens had a machine gun. If I kept the range right, he wouldn't have a clear shot at me with the MAC-10. It would be like trying to shoot down a hummingbird during a firefight.

His grenades were another matter. Those were a big problem. All he would have to do was get close enough to lob one. We had no answer for those and no equalizer.

That was the most important thing I learned during my Special Forces training: Know your enemy's capabilities just as well as your own capabilities. The old-time Green Berets used to drum that phrase into us again and again. If you know your own strengths but not your enemy's, you have at best a fifty-fifty chance of coming out on top. If you know your enemy's but you aren't sure of your own, you have a fifty-fifty chance. But if you've done your homework and you know both sides of the equation, you have a much better shot at prevailing.

I'd been on this guy's trail so long that I felt I *knew* Stephens. I understood his capabilities. I knew what weapons he had, and I knew where he was.

I had been to the firing range on several occasions and let the range master shoot several of the machine guns I had seized in ATF operations. He was a gun nut and loved shooting the exotic weapons I had. I figured he would let me use the range even on a Saturday. But when I arrived, there was no one around and the place was locked up.

I was running out of time to get my AR-15 zeroed in; I needed to find another firing range fast. I decided to make my way to the Lytle Creek outdoor range. Lytle Creek wasn't actually a firing range, just a place where people took their guns to shoot. It was pretty informal and not exactly legal. Folks brought their own targets, which often consisted of empty bottles and cans. The place was unsupervised, with people firing everything from BB guns to 50-caliber stuff. It wasn't the most advantageous place to zero my AR in, but it would have to do. I swung back to my house for a stiff cardboard box and a black Magic Marker and made my way to Lytle Creek. Shooting firearms anywhere near a residential area would almost always bring a call from local law enforcement, but Lytle Creek was kind of a sanctuary for gunslingers. There had been a number of accidental shootings up there simply because it was unsupervised. But it gave all the gun nuts a place to shoot besides their backyards.

It wouldn't take me long to get the AR zeroed. Probably six or eight shots should do it. I rolled onto the little dirt road that led down into the shooting area. The brush had been cleared on either side of the road so people could park their cars. Lytle

Creek had a few open areas among the scrub brush and rocks where people had set up targets. The ground was littered with the shattered brown and green glass of beer bottles that people had used for makeshift targets.

I found a secluded area away from everyone else. I used the Magic Marker to draw a bull's-eye on the cardboard box and then got to work. It took me eight shots before I had my rifle zeroed. I'd packed up the gun and made my way back to my car when I heard the unmistakable ripping sound of a machine gun being fired. *Holy shit,* I thought. *What now?*

I decided not to put the AR back in the trunk, but to keep it beside me while making my way out of the area. The ATF lawman in me took hold, and I was determined to find out who was in possession of the machine gun. Should I call in help? There was no way I would be able to call for backup, but there was also no way I was going to forget it and leave. I laid my service revolver on the seat beside me and chambered a round in my AR. I then started up the Mustang and began to make my way toward the area where I'd heard the machine gun, rolling past several groups of people who had AR-15s, M1s, Mini-14s, and other types of rifles. Any of them could have been converted to fire fully automatic.

No one made a move with their guns. Unless they were extremely stupid, nobody was going to brazenly fire a fully automatic weapon in front of someone they didn't know. If I stopped to watch them, I would be obvious as hell. I kept rolling slowly out of the area and didn't hear the machine gun go off again.

My mission was accomplished at Lytle Creek, and I wanted to

get home. I still had a lot of planning ahead of me. It would have been too difficult for one ATF agent to hold fifty gunslingers at bay to uncover one machine gunner. Not to mention the danger.

I began to make my way back home to Corona, but before I got farther than a mile, something pulled me toward Rancho Cucamonga. I had to make at least a pass by the wash before I went home. I turned off the 10 freeway onto Archibald and headed north; at Archibald and Base Line, I had a clear shot at the wash and the foot of the mountain. I made my way to the entrance of the drain where I had spent so much time over the last couple of months.

As I stared up at the mountains, I was seeing it all play out like a movie—what was going to happen on those trails in a few days. I sat thinking for over a couple of minutes before snapping back to the present. As I pulled away, I thought that maybe I should take a final swing past Stephens's parents' place, but I decided to head straight home.

The plan was set. I was as secure in my mind as I could be. I only needed to put the operation into action.

When I got home, I went right to work putting my equipment together: ALICE pack, flashlight, canteen, binoculars, ammo, magazines, meals ready to eat (MREs). I'd get the rest of what I needed on Monday. I took my AR from the car and began to break it down.

Cleaning a weapon had never seemed so important to me, not since my days in Vietnam. After I'd thoroughly inspected and cleaned the AR, my service revolver got the same careful treatment. I rounded up all my pictures and evidence for the presentation on Monday, and I pulled out my cammies and boots.

I had it all together. But I would wonder for the rest of the weekend if I was forgetting something, if I was leaving anything to chance. The images of Stephens—wielding his MAC-10, shoving his pistol in people's faces—and the vivid details of the police reports ran through my head until I fell asleep that night.

On Sunday morning my mix of excitement and concern hit a fever pitch. I called Wayne at home to shoot the shit.

"You ready, Wayne? I know I don't need to ask, but I'm asking."

"Sure, Billy."

"You got enough ammo?"

"Oh, yeah."

"And we're in agreement about Stephens, right?" I said. "If he makes a move, it's over with. Remember what Jimmy said? 'He's going to blow you out of your fuckin' socks.' Far as I'm concerned, he's never going to get the chance."

"I'm with you," Wayne said.

We were in total agreement on one thing. If someone died on this operation, it was *not* going to be a cop. Wayne said he was looking forward to the challenge. I was glad I'd called him; I always felt better after talking with Wayne.

Monday morning rolled around, and I was in the office by five A.M. I caught up on some paper and typed up the ops plan. I made copies of the plan and other information I thought the team members would need, and then I sat back and ran through my checklist.

The briefing was at nine A.M., and I wanted to have my shit together. Chuck Pratt was the first to make it to the office after me, and I went right up to his desk.

He grinned at me. "Queen, you got your shit together?"

"I got it all together, Chuck."

"I don't want another truckload of explosives in a high school parking lot."

Neither did I. "I got all the bases covered," I said. "The team's ready. I'm ready. Chuck, are you?"

"I'm ready," he said. "Let me hear your plan before anyone else gets here."

I ran through the details of the ops plan for him.

"Simple as that." Pratt smiled.

I didn't talk to him about the extraction; taking Stephens into custody was my greatest concern. Getting him out of the hills hadn't really crossed my mind. I figured that we would walk back down from the hills, however long it took, with the fugitive in our custody.

Pratt asked me what type of weapons I thought we should be taking in.

"I'm taking an AR-15," I said. "A worst-case scenario calls for it."

"Shotguns?"

"A shotgun at a hundred yards isn't going to be much good, and if Stephens does spot us, I'm sure he won't want to stand and fight. He's going to slip away into the brush. I want something that'll be good at a distance."

Pratt agreed but said that he wanted close-in equipment also. I didn't have a problem with that. Everyone else would be carrying shotguns with slugs and double-aught buck.

"We'll make sure everyone is covered for a two-day operation," Pratt said.

"We're taking Howard for communications and security for our base camp."

"Sounds good to me," Pratt said. "Everything is covered with Skopeck. I don't know what you said to him, Queen, but he's up for it. So far, so good."

It was nice to hear that the brass was behind the operation.

By nine A.M. all the guys were present, hanging out and waiting for the briefing to start. Pratt and I met with Wayne Morrison, Lanny Royer, Ken Cates, Howard Sanders, and Steve Kilgore in Pratt's office. All along I had been attempting to make the impression to my team members that this wasn't going to be anything close to a normal arrest. I'd have one more shot before we got knee-deep in Stephens's backyard.

We moved to the squad bay area for the briefing. I opened with a character description of Stephens. "He's extremely violent. He's got a sound history of violence, and I've been advised by people who know him well that if he catches us sneaking into his area of operation he won't have a problem shooting us. Does everyone understand that?"

Although I received the requisite nods and grunts of acknowledgment, I still wasn't convinced they completely understood, aside from Wayne Morrison.

"Guys, this is the way we're going to carry out the operation," I said. "It's going down this Wednesday. We'll have to set up a base camp on Tuesday evening. Chuck, Steve, Lanny, and Ken, you guys will make up the extraction team. Howard, you will maintain the base camp and relay radio calls from there. Wayne and I will recon into the mountains Tuesday evening and move as close to Stephens's camp as possible before night sets in. Then we'll start to move to the camp before first light. We hope to make it to Stephens's camp before he wakes up.

"At first light," I continued, "the extraction team will start moving up the mountain, led by Steve. He knows the area and how to get up the mountain. Hopefully, we can surround Stephens with a show of force that will make him give up without a fight. I say 'hopefully.' Do not expect that to be the most likely scenario.

"Everyone will need to take food and water for two days. There is a clear mountain stream that runs out of the hills, but we don't know how clean that water actually is. So fill up your canteens. Gentlemen, I can't stress this enough: Carry *plenty* of ammunition. We're in his backyard. We have no backup. We need total dominance in terms of firepower.

"San Bernardino SWAT will be on standby. But there is no

place to land a helicopter on that mountain. Don't think that Berdoo will be coming in to bail us out if things go south, gentlemen. Stephens will probably respond with machine-gun fire and with hand grenades. So far he hasn't shown any reluctance to use his machine gun on people."

The room was quiet. All of the guys had serious stares—not a facial muscle twitched. I had finally gotten through to them.

"Tuesday night will be a cold camp," I went on. "No fires and no lights. We have only one nightscope, and Wayne and I will be taking it with us on Tuesday evening. There will most likely be booby traps along the trail—this guy is known to have set them. Chuck, Wayne, and I dealt with plenty of booby traps in Vietnam. So, Steve, listen to what Chuck has to say. Move slow.

"We know that Stephens has at least six hand grenades. We know he's got plenty of ammo for those MAC-10s. Getting Stephens is important, guys, but not important enough for any of us to get hurt. I want this guy in cuffs and all *seven* of the people in this room coming back down that mountain in one piece. Anybody got any questions?"

I waited. The room was still dead quiet. The mood was set for the operation.

Chuck Pratt told everyone to take the rest of the day to get mentally prepped for tomorrow. We'd all be meeting at my house and then move to base camp from there. As the meeting broke up and people filed out, reality hit me for the first time.

It was going down. What other agencies hadn't been able to complete, we were going to do. What two SWAT teams had tried and failed, we were going to accomplish. I knew it in my gut.

After the team members were all gone, I made my way to the tech office and picked up the nightscope. It was an old Vietnam-era scope, cumbersome and fragile, but it worked fine. I knew we'd be needing it in that mountain darkness. I picked up fire-flies—small strobe lights that are used as locating devices—in case the shit went bad. Pratt would pick up MREs and distribute them to the team tomorrow. Everything was ready. I headed home.

As always, we'd plan for the worst and hope for the best. The element of surprise was our big advantage; the smart guys will always hit you when you least expect it. Stephens knew the cops were after him. He had been in the hills for five years, and no one had managed to nab him. He was comfortable and might even have become complacent. At least that was what I figured.

I knew the terrain, and what it would take to reach Stephens's camp, after learning from the mistakes Fontana and San Bernardino had made. They'd tried to make it happen in a one-day operation; I knew we had to factor in at least a day and a half of climbing, due to the hazards of the terrain and the weather. I planned on an all-day trek, a quick night's sleep, and then several more hours of hiking to reach Stephens's location. If everything went according to plan, Wayne and I would be in his camp before sunup and catch him unaware. He'd be unable to go for his weapons before my AR was in his face.

Communication was our biggest weakness. I knew from my time chasing Stephens around in the valley how poor radio communication was there, so to compensate, we would set up a relay station at the foot of the mountain.

I had briefed Berdoo SWAT captain Mike Cardwell so his team would be on standby at the air support hangar in Rialto. The weather didn't look like it would be a problem, although we would go in no matter what. But we would have to be prepared for temperatures ranging anywhere from the low fifties to the low hundreds.

The one factor I had the most confidence in was that Wayne Morrison and I had the same Green Beret training. I knew we could keep cool and improvise under fire.

Our Special Forces training at Fort Bragg had been no joke. Sleep deprivation and long-movement exercises could take several days. We jumped from airplanes and helicopters and learned how to fire everything from a Colt 1911 .45-caliber pistol to a LAW rocket. Hand-to-hand combat and survival skills were drilled into us until they became second nature. I'd spent plenty of time training in the Uwharrie National Forest, learning how to move using cover without getting caught.

"Camouflage is an art," I remember one training sergeant telling me. "You gotta look like your environment. You gotta look like a tree or a bush or the ground. If you don't, when you come up against the Vietcong, they're going to kill you."

At Fort Bragg, we didn't want to fail or let our trainers

down, but I didn't have to worry about someone putting a bullet through me. Our trainers did their best to drill into us how important it was for us to be survivors who relied on our wits. "If you don't learn how to do this," they screamed at us over and over again, "you're going to die in Vietnam." I didn't realize how important training was until I was over in Vietnam. Many times in that jungle warfare, I thanked those Fort Bragg trainers for the hell they put us through.

But this wasn't a training exercise. This was for real. One fuckup would mean a bullet in the brain; a haphazard step on a trip wire connected to an IED or some other type of booby trap meant losing a leg, if not my life. Even more sobering was the fact that I had gotten my ATF friends involved. I had to do that much more preparation, since it wasn't just my life on the line.

Over the past few days, Wayne had been as stone-faced as I was. He knew the threat Stephens posed. But the other members of the team still worried me. I feared they really didn't understand. As much as I had tried to drill it in their heads, I knew I sounded like one of my trainers back at Fort Bragg. All the warnings in the world weren't going to mean shit until you walked the walk.

My AR-15 was ready. The scope was zeroed. I had four thirty-round and eight twenty-round magazines taped together in twos. ATF agents carried revolvers back in the eighties, so I had another fifty rounds of ammunition for my six-shooter. The last thing I wanted was to run out of ammunition. I packed food and water for two days, medical supplies, radios. I was sure Stephens was ready for war. I wanted to be as ready as he was.

Tuesday came, and the team met at my house right before noon. The next two days were forecasted to be clear and hot.

After our quick rendezvous, I looked them each in the eye as we all headed out.

"This ain't no game, boys," I said. "This is for real. Think on it hard. There is more than a damn good chance that this guy is going to want to shoot it out with us. You remember what I said."

Everyone was quiet as I spoke. I hoped I'd made an impression.

Sixteen

At approximately four P.M. we arrived at the base camp at the foot of the mountain. Chuck Pratt and the extraction team, along with Howard Sanders, began setting up camp for the evening, while Wayne and I readied ourselves for the evening recon, using ground-up charcoal to cammy up our faces. Steve Kilgore and the U.S. Forest Service had furnished the team radios, which they'd checked and rechecked. If things went bad for Wayne and me on recon, the radio was our sole contact to the outside world.

At approximately four-thirty, Wayne and I said our good-byes and started our climb into the mountains. We were hauling a lot of equipment, but we were both in good shape. We knew what we were up against, so we moved slowly and deliberately. Initially, the terrain was steep, with rough vegetation about waist-high, and about thirty minutes into the climb, we began to hit obstacles. The wild scrub-oak brush was about six to seven feet tall and thick enough to keep us from walking upright. We used sign-cutting techniques to follow Stephens's trail, moving on our hands and knees under the chaparral.

After a few hours of crawling, Wayne and I made our way to the edge of a canyon where it looked like Stephens had fixed a rope to rappel down to a deer trail that ran along the canyon wall. It was tough not to feel vertigo; at times we were as high as two hundred feet above the canyon floor. Wayne and I began to rappel in a bounding-over watch mode: I covered him as he rapelled down the rope, and then he covered me. We stayed in motion at all times, looking for Stephens on the trail. We also were always on the watch for the booby traps and IEDs that Jimmy had warned us about.

Our movements were slow but steady. We followed Stephens's trail to the bottom of the canyon, where a clear stream ran out of the mountains. I was glad to see that little creek—moving along a stream gives you good noise cover, so you can move faster. We crossed the stream several times, following the trail until it got so dark that we had to slow to a crawl. The sun set, and the temperature dropped drastically. When we'd left the base camp, the temperature had been in the mid-nineties, but we had climbed several thousand feet, the sun had gone down, and the air was brisk and cold. I hadn't fully expected the temperature to go as low as it did.

For nearly an hour we tried to make progress in the darkness. But then we agreed it was best to stop. We had moved as far as we could at night without running the serious risk of tripping a booby trap. Stephens wouldn't be moving at this time of the night, so it was time for us to lie down and get some rest.

Back at base camp, Chuck Pratt and the guys had staked out their sleeping areas. Howard Sanders had brought his military sleeping bag and laid it out in the back of his pickup truck. Howard wasn't what you would call a mountain man; he didn't even like to camp. Sometime in the night, he started to freak out. He'd watched enough *Wild Kingdom* that he was sure he'd heard something bad coming out of the wilderness. Curled up in his sleeping bag, zipped to his neck, he held his gun in hand. He couldn't sleep, waiting for the attack bears or coyotes or Bigfoot. Suddenly, Howard spotted something. Bright eyes in the brush.

A deer jumped from the bushes and ran through the camp, and Howard stood straight up in his bag, dropping his gun at his feet, where it fell loudly on the flatbed of the pickup. The sound woke the whole arrest-and-extraction team, who sat up in their sleeping bags, cursing and groaning, yelling at Howard. Howard grumbled back, looking for his pistol in the darkness. As far as he was concerned, this was above and beyond the call of duty.

Back up on the mountain, the temperature had dropped so low, and I was shivering so much, that I thought about curling up with my Green Beret buddy to conserve body heat. If we'd been going by the Special Forces playbook, we would have done that right away, but something kept us from sharing sleeping quarters. We would have been a lot more comfortable if we had put that macho bullshit aside, though. I tried to sleep, but the cold wind was howling, and the realization that Stephens was close by kept me wide awake. I ran scenarios of the upcoming confrontation through my head.

Wayne wasn't sleeping much, either, but we continued to lie on the trail, resting our bodies and our eyes. At approximately three A.M. Wayne and I agreed that we could move by the light of the moon as long as we went slowly. We began inching our way up the mountain. After about an hour, I picked up Stephens's trail again. He had climbed the canyon wall to a deer trail, which he followed farther up the mountain. The farther we went, the more discernible the trail got. Stephens had slashed vegetation away from parts of the trail, making it easier for us to follow.

But I knew that the closer we got to Stephens's camp, the more likely we were to be stepping on trip wires and booby traps, either early-warning or anti-personnel devices. The latter was obviously more troubling. Jimmy had said he'd helped Stephens booby-trap the trail himself.

I could feel it—we were close. It was time to stop and unload some of our equipment. I signaled to Wayne, and we dumped all the nonessentials into the brush. We headed on, carrying only what we needed to communicate and to go into battle.

It was just after four A.M. when we made it to the jagged mountain ridge. The area above us had been roughly cleared. I took another cautious step forward.

The night was now pitch-black; the moon had disappeared behind the clouds that had moved in. My heart began to race as I remembered Jimmy's warning: *He's gonna blow you outta your fuckin' socks.* I took another step and heard a light crunching of twigs and rocks under my boot heel—and then the outline of camouflaged canvas came into view. Fluttering like a flag, Stephens's tent was only inches in front of me, close enough to grab.

I stood dead still, my head thumping with adrenaline and fear, realizing that the criminal I'd been stalking for months was barely six feet away from me, somewhere inside the tent.

Had Stephens heard us approach? Was he, at this very second, pulling the pin on one of his grenades, or had he opted for the machine gun? I inched my finger to the selector switch on my AR-15 and moved it to fire. Just the faintest metallic click. But in the cold silence of that mountaintop, it sounded like I'd fired a round.

I signaled for Wayne, a few strides to my rear, to stop advancing. He quickly moved to the flank. I lowered my AR to cover him as he silently moved away.

I took a few steps away from Stephens's tent, my eyes straining in the darkness, looking for cover. I needed a few moments to collect myself, to pull together an improvised ops plan to take

Stephens into custody if he exited the tent before Chuck Pratt and the arrest-and-extraction team made it to the camp. After a few steps through the darkness, I reached behind me and felt a sharp outcrop of granite surrounded by a couple of scrawny bushes.

A pale purple dawn was starting to break. The half-light allowed me to survey the campsite. Mark Stephens was a savvy mountain man: He'd selected his position perfectly. The tent was on the crest of a canyon cliff that had a clear line of sight on any approaching intruders below. Chuck Pratt and his team would be making the trip right through Stephens's sights at any moment.

I had to warn them. But how? Using the radio was out of the question, and I'd already taken a huge chance making my AR hot. The squelch from a radio would surely wake Stephens. And sending Wayne Morrison back down the hill would be just as risky. The daylight was getting brighter by the moment, and the increased visibility was working against us.

As I turned to get Wayne's attention, I caught a glimpse of Lanny Royer jumping the creek down in the canyon. My focus shot back to the tent. If Stephens exited now, he'd see the extraction team for sure. They'd be coming at him like penny-arcade targets; he'd calmly pick them off one by one with his rifle.

I was clear about one thing: If Mark Stephens exited the tent now, there would be no handcuffs, no tussling, no reciting of his Miranda rights. I'd have to blow him away.

Suddenly, I heard rustling from inside the tent.

"Shit, man," a gruff voice said. "We gotta get up."

Then, to my complete shock, came a second, deeper voice.

"Shut the fuck up, man. Go back to sleep."

Jesus Christ. I turned to Wayne and signaled: *Two black hats in the tent.* I saw Wayne grip his rifle and focus in. The taut canvas trembled, and the front flap flew open. I ducked farther down behind the slab of sandstone. There was no time to formulate a plan of action. We would have to wing it on pure lawman instinct.

Stephens crawled out of the tent with a Colt pistol in hand. He straightened up, strapped on a holster, and tucked the gun on his hip. Then he disappeared in the brush behind his tent. Could he flank us? Would he accidentally stumble on the backup team? And who was his partner—what kind of arms did he have?

The worst-case scenario for a law enforcement takedown operation is to lose control of the variables. Here we were in Stephens's backyard—his own patch of high-altitude wilderness—and we'd lost control of the situation. I signaled Wayne to cover our flank as I waited for Stephens's partner to exit the tent.

Stephens stumbled back into the camp. He'd only gathered a pile of dry branches for a fire, but my relief was momentary. Stephens scratched his beard and turned, walking straight toward me. I gripped my AR-15, finger resting on the trigger. Stephens stopped just short of the outcrop. He unzipped his fly, sighed, and let loose with a steaming stream of urine. Even homicidal survivalists need to take their morning piss.

I had to regain control before the hunters became the hunted. As Stephens walked off to gather more firewood, my eyes flashed back and forth: tent, hill, tent, hill. Just then I saw Chuck Pratt slipping into the perimeter, and I knew that the other agents would be close behind. I signaled to Pratt that we had two bad guys to deal with—one in the tent, one up the hill. Pratt nodded, turning and signaling to the other ATF agents. Life-and-death communication was being accomplished through military sign language—rudimentary but effective.

Stephens walked back into the camp with more wood. Then, for no apparent reason, he dropped the wood and walked straight toward me. *Fuck it, that's it,* I told myself, tightening the grip on my AR-15. I jumped up and leveled the assault rifle at Stephens: "Police! *Freeze! Freeze!*"

Stephens's eyes flashed wildly, filled with rage at being taken by surprise. In one fluid movement, as he locked his fearless gaze on mine, his right hand went for the pistol on his side. I squeezed the trigger on my assault rifle. In a shattering instant, all hell broke loose. The cool mountain air exploded in gunfire from three ATF assault rifles . . .

Seventeen

Stephens went for his gun and jumped for cover behind an outcrop, all in one smooth athletic movement. We could hardly see him in the dim light—he was just a faint outline, making for a difficult moving target.

Wayne Morrison, Chuck Pratt, and I all opened up on Stephens at the same time. It was sheer chaos. Bullets were whizzing blindly, flying from different trajectories. The echoing rifle reports bounced off the canyon walls and seemed to surround us. No one knew for certain who was firing. Was Stephens's partner opening up on us, too?

Other ATF agents were shouting, cursing, diving for cover

behind rocks. Everyone began taking up positions, expecting a prolonged shoot-out.

Our initial volley of shots blew by Stephens. A few rounds hit the rock he was hiding behind and echoed across the mountaintop.

Then Stephens did the one thing I hadn't anticipated. From behind his slab of rock, he started hollering: "I give up! I give up!"

I was stunned. I didn't believe him at first. Was it a trap? A fake surrender so he could get a clear shot at one of us?

"Stand up!" I commanded. "Drop the gun and put your hands over your head!"

But Stephens refused to get up.

"Stand up, Stephens!" I shouted. "Let's see your hands!"

Again and again he refused. Maybe he didn't believe we were cops.

"If I get up, you're gonna shoot me," he said.

Chuck Pratt and I took turns hollering out orders. We shouted to Stephens that we were ATF agents, that we'd come with a warrant to arrest him, not shoot him in cold blood.

It took quite a bit of reassurance before Stephens was convinced that we weren't going to kill him. At last he decided to stand. He set down his pistol and emerged with his hands in the air.

When the smoke cleared, Chuck Pratt and Wayne Morrison moved in on Stephens to secure him. Ken Cates and I rushed toward the tent to clear it.

Ken was screaming as we approached: "You in the tent! Come out with your hands up!"

Ken picked up a rock and threw it at the tent. Nothing. We cautiously made our way to the front of the tent, pointing our weapons. I was shocked when I bent over to look into the tent and saw that no one was inside.

I began scanning the area for someone who may have slipped out while we were occupied with Stephens. When nothing turned up, Lanny Royer and Steve Kilgore made a quick sweep of the area. I made my way back to where Wayne and Pratt had Stephens in handcuffs.

"Where's your buddy?" I asked Stephens.

"What the hell are you talking about?" he replied.

"The guy in the tent with you," I said. "The one you were talking to right when you got up this morning. Where is he?"

"Man, that was me," he said. "I talk to myself like that all the time."

"You sure about that?"

"There ain't nobody else up here," he said.

My heart was still pumping hard. I went back to the tent. There was only one sleeping bag inside.

"Shit," I said. "He really was talking to himself."

Things started to settle down.

Pratt sounded off. "Is everybody okay?" he shouted. "Nobody's got any holes in them, right?"

Everybody answered back that they were all right.

"Okay," Pratt said. He picked up a radio and called Howard Sanders. "Sanders, Pratt."

"Go ahead, Pratt."

"We are code four up here. But relay to the division that we were involved in a shooting with the suspect."

In a freak moment of atmospheric clarity on that mountaintop, the radio transmitted clear down in the valley. Skopeck, in his car heading for the office downtown, actually heard the transmission. Within seconds, he radioed back. "Are all our guys okay?"

"Yes, sir, Mr. Skopeck," Pratt responded. "The suspect didn't want to give up and challenged us to a gunfight. But he thought better of it in short order. Nobody was hit, sir."

I moved back to where Stephens was being guarded at gunpoint by Steve Kilgore and Lanny Royer. The anger and hatred had vanished from his face; he seemed subdued, resigned to the reality of his capture. Pratt stepped in and asked Stephens why he'd tried to draw on me after I had identified myself as the police. Stephens said that he'd seen me and Wayne, and while clean-cut Morrison looked like a cop, I, with my long, curly hair, looked more like some kind of drug-crazed hippie. He'd thought I was coming to steal his dope.

We fanned out to search Stephens's area of operation and found four separate marijuana fields containing hundreds of plants, most of which were over six feet tall. Some towered as high as ten and twelve feet. I was stunned at the size of the plants. I was also amazed at the work that had been put into the operation. I advised Stephens of his Miranda rights and told him that he was under arrest for growing marijuana on federal land and for possession of machine guns and hand grenades.

He nodded and grunted in response when I asked if he understood his rights. His eyes were blank, as if he were a hundred miles away, as if this were all happening to someone else.

Glancing around the camp, I saw a set of barbells. "How the hell did you get a set of barbells up here?"

Stephens responded as if it were no big deal. "I humped them up."

I tallied the iron plates. There were 190 pounds of free weights sitting there. Having just made the climb myself—rappelling down cliff faces, crossing slippery streams and jagged outcrops—I had to marvel at the superhuman level of his conditioning.

Steve Kilgore had radioed his people at the U.S. Forest Service and advised them of the size of the marijuana fields. When Stephens was secured, I began to survey the camp area myself. Kilgore informed us that the Forest Service wanted all the marijuana plants cut down. Since we were already here, they reasoned, we might as well save them another airdrop by chopping down the pot plantation, and preserve the chain of custody by bringing the evidence down from the mountain with us. By now the sun was up, and the heat was quickly becoming intense. We hacked and hacked at the massive marijuana plants as the temperature climbed into the nineties. But no one complained about the heat as we bundled and carried the plants from the fields that Stephens had so meticulously maintained.

When I stopped for a moment to catch my breath, I caught sight of something that sent a chill up my spine. Way down below us, a cloud of smoke was rising from the foot of the mountain.

"Shit," I said. "We didn't make it this far to be burned alive in a firestorm."

I got on the radio and asked John Carenco, an ATF agent who was manning a secure area at the U.S. Forest Service compound, if he could see the fire from his position.

"Hell, yeah, I see it," said Carenco.

Any thoughts of humping back down that mountain with our prisoner in tow went up in smoke.

We had only one way out now. Tom Federoff.

I told Carenco to get in touch with Federoff at the Berdoo Sheriff's Department and tell him we needed him to get us the hell out of here. I let everyone know in short order that we would be choppering off the mountain as soon as we could get a bird up here. Handcuffed on the ground, Stephens overheard what I was saying.

"Am I going to have to fly out of here, too?" he asked. It was the first time he'd seemed genuinely engaged in the process of his arrest.

I told Stephens that we couldn't leave him up here; he was under arrest and would be choppered out with us. Stephens must have had a deadly fear of helicopters, because he started begging. It seemed pretty ironic to me that this tough guy who'd spent years terrorizing the towns of the Inland Empire was now sitting before me, scared out of his wits. He pleaded with us not to take him out by helicopter. He swore that he would walk down and meet us at the bottom of the mountain.

To my surprise, Lanny Royer spoke up and said that he would walk down with Stephens. I stared at Lanny. "You, too?"

Lanny didn't seem to be afraid of the devil himself. I mean, I had once watched him, during a heated argument, almost knock Mort Jacobson's lights out in the middle of the street. And now he was afraid of a little chopper ride?

Stephens was doing his best to negotiate. He said we could tie a rope around his neck, dangle the rope from the helicopter, and he would walk down under the chopper.

"I don't think so," I said. Still, I could understand their concern.

I began running contingency plans past Pratt. We figured that the helicopter was our only viable route of escape.

"Federoff gets us off this mountain, or we may not be getting off," I said, looking down at the black and gray smoke clouds billowing below.

I asked Stephens if there was another way off the mountain other than the way we'd come, and what it was like going toward the top from where we were. Stephens said we could forget that idea. It would be harder climbing the rest of the way to the top of the mountain than trying to skirt around the fire.

I keyed the radio again. "Sanders. Queen," I yelled. "Were you able to get in touch with the Berdoo air wing?"

"I did," Howard said. "Federoff says that he'll get you up on the radio when he gets airborne."

It couldn't have been another five minutes before I heard my radio crack. "ATF—Queen—can you copy?"

"Go ahead, Tom," I said.

"I'm inbound to see what the air is like up there. I'll see if it's gonna take some kind of miracle to get you guys out of there.

But don't worry, Queen. Whatever it takes, I'll get you off that hill."

Federoff's confidence was reassuring. And I knew what kind of skills he had with his bird. The radio crackled again.

"Say, Queen, is there any place we can set a small chopper down up there?"

"No way in hell," I said. "You might be able to sling us out. Spy-roping would work for me, but some of the guys up here are a bit nervous about just getting on a chopper." Spy-roping is a technique in which a rope is dropped from a chopper that's hovering above. You hook onto the rope using a D-ring. The helicopter then lifts you out. You make the trip dangling from the rope under the chopper.

"We'll get you out," Federoff assured me. "Don't worry, my friend."

But we couldn't help but worry. I remembered Federoff telling me that heat, altitude, and mountains were a precarious combination. Now we were tossing in a forest fire for good measure. Before we'd experienced the rabbit trails, deer trails, jagged cliffs, and canyon walls, we'd been planning on walking back out, even if one guy was in handcuffs. Now any other way out sounded good to me.

I could hear the distant thunder of the chopper blades approaching. Soon I got a look at Federoff as he swung in. He was flying a Hughes 500, which is a small four-man helicopter. The radio crackled again. "ATF—Queen—this is Federoff."

"Go ahead, Tom."

"Queen, can you pop smoke and show us where you are? I

mean without burning the rest of the mountain down. It's already cooking from down below."

"You got it," I said. I had one canister of yellow smoke. I found a clearing and popped the canister. "I'm popping yellow smoke," I radioed.

In a few seconds he responded, "I see yellow smoke."

The chopper continued its thunderous approach.

"Okay, Tom. That's us. Now get us the hell out of here."

"Okay, Queen, I seem to be able to move around here pretty good. We just need to find a place where we can get close enough to the ground to get you guys on board."

"We're gonna need to get grass and equipment out of here also. Is a sling-load operation out of the question?" A sling is a net you haul equipment in that is hooked to the bottom of the chopper. When the net has equipment in it, it is called a sling load.

"Sling-loading's going to be easier than getting you guys in a chopper."

"Sounds good to me," I said. I thought back to a helicopter jump I had made while with Special Forces near Fort Bragg. A good friend of mine, Sergeant Speed, had gotten hung up on a skid while making a parachute jump. He couldn't get air underneath the chopper for some reason, and it nearly killed him.

Still, sling-loading sounded better than being burned alive. In moments Federoff was directly overhead, circling around us.

"Queen," Federoff said, "I can drop a sling into the area where the marijuana is and pick up the dope and equipment first. I see a cliff not far from your location. If you guys can make it to the edge of that cliff, I can probably hover close enough to get you on board."

I knew Stephens and Lanny wouldn't want anything to do with this operation. But the smoke at the bottom of the mountain was growing thicker and more ominous. "We'll do it," I answered.

"Okay, Queen, I'm heading back up to the airport to pick up a slick," Federoff said. A slick is what we called a UH-1D type of helicopter, also known as a Huey, during the Vietnam War.

"Hurry back," I said.

I gathered everyone around me and announced the plan. I told them we'd need to get the grass and the equipment to the closest marijuana field. Berdoo SWAT would drop in a sling, and we'd fill it with the grass first and then our radios, guns, and night vision equipment.

It was getting hotter by the minute. In the distance below, I could see tongues of flame leaping from the burning forest. As soon as we had gathered the marijuana and equipment, Federoff was there with the sling. He swooped in with his slick, and we quickly loaded the first sling with the marijuana. Memories of Vietnam flooded back again as I watched the chopper pulling away.

Federoff was back in ten minutes, and we made the second sling load of our guns and equipment. The air was getting smokier, and I was getting more nervous about the heat and fire. Federoff was, too.

"Listen up," I told everyone. "We're going to have to move to the edge of that cliff to get on the helicopter."

The cliff was about ninety feet—probably high enough to

break legs, necks, and backs. I went over to the edge of the cliff first, hoping to give the others more confidence about boarding the chopper. I wasn't considering what it might do to their confidence if I took a dive into the canyon.

We didn't have much time, with the fire below fast approaching, but it wasn't long before I heard the chopper. We stood near the edge of the cliff, watching Federoff maneuver the helicopter closer and closer to the edge. There was no way he would get his chopper over the ground, and a large dead tree kept him from reaching the edge of the cliff.

We had no choice. We would all have to jump and grab the loadmaster, skids, whatever we could reach, and pull ourselves in.

I didn't want to think about it too much. I knew if we had any hope of getting off the mountain in one piece, I'd have to lead by example.

As soon as the chopper got close enough to the edge of the cliff, I took a couple of steps and jumped. The rushing air swept around me like a vortex. The view was dizzying, and the canyon floor below me looked like a drop of miles. I seemed to hang in the air for an eternity before the loadmaster reached out and grabbed me. I hung on for dear life, pulling myself onto the floor of the chopper.

"Jesus! That was close!" I said.

I turned and looked at what Federoff was dealing with. His feet and hands were working furiously as he flew that chopper for all it was worth. The main rotor was turning only inches from the dead tree. There was zero margin for error.

Federoff didn't have any time to say hello, and although I

wanted to give him a big kiss, I figured I could wait till we landed. I made my way back to the door. Stephens was standing on the cliff with his hands cuffed in front. Wayne and Pratt took him by the arms and legs and led him right to the edge of the cliff.

Stephens was still pleading with us not to take him by air, but he also seemed to know we were throwing his ass on that chopper, so he might as well not put up a struggle. One-two-three-go: They somehow managed to toss the two-hundred-pound Stephens up to me and the loadmaster.

Lanny Royer was next up. Lanny was a pretty religious guy—not exactly a holy roller but certainly the most churchgoing one among the team. He was whispering prayers to Jesus, Mary, and every single one of the apostles, with a look of terror frozen on his face as he got ready to make his leap. He jumped, and the loadmaster and I grabbed his arms and legs and pulled him in. I looked up to see Federoff still fighting mightily to keep the chopper off the cliff and its rotors out of the dead tree.

The chopper had room for ten men in back, but Federoff didn't want to push his luck. He figured he'd make two trips. He began to back away from the cliff, turned toward the valley floor, and took us down. The rotor wash was blowing air through the chopper like a giant fan. I wanted to let out a big rebel yell but thought I'd wait until we were all safe down in the valley. Lanny didn't look like he was up for any celebrations. Mark Stephens wasn't going to be doing any celebrating, either.

The Ranger camp came into view, and I saw Carenco standing there, along with a couple of ATF agents and San Bernardino cops. I had never been so glad to see my brothers in blue.

Federoff landed the chopper softer than a butterfly with sore feet. Lanny and I grabbed Stephens and hopped off the chopper.

"Hello, John," I said to Carenco. "This is Mr. Mark Stephens."

Carenco let out a laugh. He turned and pointed. "There's your stuff," he said. "It's all totaled. Your chopper pilot let it go a couple of hundred feet up. Just a test to see how well it was constructed. It didn't do too well."

At first I thought he was kidding, but he insisted I go over and take a look. As Tom Federoff had been bringing the bird down the slope, he accidentally hit the release button for the sling while the chopper was still more than a hundred feet off the ground. All our gear—guns, radios, nightscope—was busted to pieces, totaled. Good thing Carenco wasn't totaled as well. ATF brass was going to pitch a bitch about the expense. *Big deal,* I told myself, *big fuckin' deal.* We'd gotten out of a shoot-out. We had Mark Stephens in custody. And we were all coming home from the operation alive. A few scrapes and scratches, but no one was too much worse for the wear. (No one except Lanny Royer, that is. Up on the mountain, during the shoot-out with Stephens, Lanny had taken cover in a patch of poison ivy. He ended up covered in a fiery, blistering rash and was hospitalized in the days ahead with one of the worst cases of poison ivy I've ever seen.)

In short order, the chopper returned with the rest of the team. I looked back up at the mountain and watched in satisfied silence as tanker planes dive-bombed the hills with fire retardant.

Eighteen

Up on the mountain, while we were waiting for Tom Federoff to come get us, I had time to talk to Mark Stephens at length. Strangely, he seemed to want to tell me all about his life in the Berdoo Mountains. It was quite a remarkable story.

I felt a little eerie questioning this fugitive I'd been trying to chase down for months. Stephens was completely calm about the whole process—chillingly calm, in fact. I tried not to let him see a glimpse of my own emotions, which were running the gamut from exhilaration to pride to sheer relief that the three-month-long chase was at last over.

Stephens's physical conditioning was astonishing—as evidenced by the fact that he'd humped a 190-pound barbell set up a mountain. He told me how he'd lived up there alone in a tent. His friends, for the most part, were animals; he got along better with them than with people—except for the badger. He said he had tried really hard to be friends with the badger, but the badger wanted nothing to do with him. After it had viciously attacked him, Stephens had shot it, skinned it, and eaten the meat.

I questioned Stephens about his dietary habits. I'd seen a lot of tin cans in his camp, but most of them were rusted and had clearly been there for a long time. He told me that at first he'd brought food from stores in the valley, but after a while he'd begun to live off the land. He'd planted and tended his own vegetables and killed wild animals for meat.

"What about water?" I asked.

He said that he'd drunk the water from the creek, and it had nearly killed him. He'd gotten so sick that he had to leave the hills and seek medical attention. The doctors told him that they suspected he had AIDS. He told them it wasn't possible, but they continued to insist that all his symptoms were consistent with the disease. He returned to the hills and continued to get sicker and sicker, losing more weight, until he was hovering near death.

He climbed back down the mountain. Finally, after a multitude of blood tests, the doctors identified a parasite in his intestines that he had ingested via the water. This story got me thinking about my team members and wondering who may have drunk the creek water. But Stephens told me that you had to drink the water on a consistent basis in order to acquire enough parasites to make you as sick as he'd gotten. He had learned that iodine would kill the parasites, so he began adding it to the water, and his problem was solved.

I also asked Stephens about his marijuana growing and other illegal activities in the valley, which I soon learned he was extremely proud of. He said that his grass was hands down the finest grown in California, and that he knew everything there was to know about growing marijuana. His four fields were manicured to perfection; he had learned to quarantine the male plants and use them only to pollinate the female plants. He had an impressive, if highly illegal, green thumb.

Stephens had once humped in a water pump and hoses to irrigate the plants, but that method hadn't worked out as well as he'd hoped. He chose to water his plants by hand, carrying countless gallons in buckets up from the creek. There was little wonder Stephens was in such fantastic shape.

But I was less interested in Stephens's physique than in the workings of his brain. Obviously, I'm not a shrink or a social worker. But I've done my share of reading on aberrant criminal psychology. The psychologist Robert Hare wrote the most widely accepted checklist for diagnosing sociopaths, who he described as "intra-species predators who use charm, manipulation, intimidation, and violence to control others and to satisfy their own selfish needs. Lacking in conscience and in feelings for others, they cold-bloodedly take what they want and do as they please, violating social norms and expectations without the slightest sense of guilt or regret."

The more I talked to Stephens, the more I realized that his

personality disorder fit the textbook definition of a sociopath. When I raised the issues of his use of violence and his possession of machine guns and hand grenades, Stephens showed no emotion at all. He just shrugged, his face blank. He said that he couldn't deal with people; they made him angry when they didn't do what he wanted them to do, and that made him want to hurt them. For him, he said, violence wasn't a big deal. It was just the best way to deal with people. He loved that sense of being in control of others, whether it was through outright violence or the threat of physical harm. He had no guilt or remorse about anyone he'd beaten up, shot, or threatened to murder.

The firearms obsession was, to Stephens, nothing but a hobby, an interesting pastime. He said he loved machine guns, and that was why he built them. When he talked about weapons, Stephens's eyes got wide, and he acted like a kid talking about his collection of Lionel trains. He told me that he had ordered the MAC-10 parts out of magazines and had built five of them. Besides the MAC-10 at the bottom of the hill, there were four more in the attic at his parents' house. He even offered to go get them for us if I wanted to see them.

But when I pressed Stephens on the subject of hand grenades, his whole demeanor changed. "I don't have anything to say about that," he said. I couldn't understand his sudden shift in behavior. What was it about the hand grenades? Possessing them wasn't any more serious a crime than owning illegal machine guns. I guess Stephens thought it might be a more serious crime. He was adamant: He wasn't sharing any information on the grenades.

"Did you know I was on the hunt for you?" I asked.

Stephens smiled a little ruefully. "Yeah, I did." He said he'd been expecting me to show up at any time.

Stephens then told me that when the gunfire started, he felt like he was in a dream. He could literally feel the bullets as they whizzed past him—tiny wind torrents rushing past his skin.

He thanked me for not killing him.

"No problem," I said.

We took Stephens in handcuffs down to Rancho Cucamonga so he could help us recover his other weapons from his parents' house. I met Mike Vaughn as we pulled up on Valley Street in front of the Stephens residence.

Mike came with us to approach Stephens's parents. Geri was visibly relieved to see her son alive. I told Geri and Russell that Mark had told us he'd secreted several other machine guns in the attic, and I asked for their consent to search the attic for the guns.

I was surprised when Russell immediately said no; he didn't want us looking there. Mike Vaughn spoke up, telling them that we would just secure the residence and get a search warrant in a few hours for the entire house if Russell didn't grant us consent to go up in the attic.

Russell changed his tune and gave Mike the okay, and I waited downstairs with everyone else. In a matter of seconds, Mike began handing down MAC-10 parts, enough to complete four more machine guns. He also searched for any other prohibited items, including ammunition, explosives, and hand grenades, but didn't find anything.

It had been a long day. The only thing left to do was book Stephens into custody. Howard Sanders and I took care of that job.

Mark Stephens was charged with multiple counts of possession of machine guns and hand grenades, but federal prosecutors allowed him to plea-bargain that charge to a single possession count. He was sentenced to five years in federal prison.

ATF headquarters in Washington, D.C., appointed a shooting review board to go to Los Angeles and make sure that our shooting on the mountain fell within Bureau guidelines. I had to make the trip back to Stephens's camp one more time to escort the suits from the review board. The mandated trip made me feel like I'd done something wrong. But the review board ultimately concluded that it had been a "good" shoot and that we'd done everything within ATF guidelines. So I managed to get over that final bureaucratic hurdle.

I spent much of the next month going back up to the hills, running all over the San Bernardino Valley, looking for the hand grenades that Stephens had constructed. We never recovered a single one.

Those hand grenades would worry me for years to come, while my time as an ATF special agent stretched into decades. I always thought about the carnage that would result from an unsuspecting child stumbling across one of those grenades, pulling the pin, and blowing up himself and God knows how many others.

I even got word to Stephens behind bars, expressing my concerns about the grenades, pleading with him to tell me their location. But Stephens was steadfast in his refusal to cooperate. It didn't make any difference to him. He said he had hidden the grenades in a place where no one would ever find them.

Epilogue

Twenty years after the arrest and prosecution of Mark Stephens, I flew back to Southern California for one last visit with my old boss on the case. Sadly, Chuck Pratt had passed away from a sudden heart attack at the age of fifty-eight, and many ATF agents, former and present, were gathering for his funeral. One of the members from the Stephens team, Lanny Royer, drove his green Dodge pickup from his home in Phoenix and picked up my current wife, Allysson, and me. It was a good hour's drive from L.A., but we got to the Garcia Mortuary in Oxnard before anyone else. I was unsure how many of the old guys would be in attendance; in the two decades since the arrest and prosecution of Stephens, the members of that team had largely scattered to the wind.

I'd retired from the Bureau of Alcohol, Tobacco and Firearms in 2003, with twenty years on the job—twenty-eight years in law enforcement—to publish and promote my first book, *Under and Alone,* a memoir of my years working undercover in the investigation of the Mongols outlaw motorcycle gang. Most of the other agents on the team had gone on to impressive careers with the feds. After years as a top-notch field agent, Wayne Morrison took a position at Bureau headquarters in Washington, D.C., where he worked for years as an ATF project manager before retiring in 2005. Ken Cates left ATF, taking a job with U.S. Customs and rising to become the special agent in charge of Dallas, Texas, where he supervised many major investigations. Howard Sanders stayed with ATF and eventually became a group supervisor with the Los Angeles Metro Group.

Lanny Royer, like Wayne Morrison, went to D.C. to work at Bureau headquarters, then came back out west, becoming a group supervisor down in San Diego. He and I crossed paths several times over the years; in the late nineties I went undercover on one of his murder-for-hire cases, posing as a hired hit man. We ended up sending two guys to prison for attempted murder. Lanny also played a major part in the ATF investigation of Jeffrey Don Lundgren, the notorious Christian cult leader and mass murderer who was executed at an Ohio prison in October 2006.

As for Chuck Pratt, he'd taken the most unlikely career path. He turned his back on the desk duties of an administrator; he was such a go-getter, he couldn't stomach the admin work as group supervisor and opted instead to go back into the field as a special agent. From the late eighties through the late nineties, he put together a ton of good cases running the gamut from narcotics and firearms busts to undercover operations against gangs and investigations targeting international gun-smuggling rings. He had recently taken a job with the L.A. Police Academy.

I never thought I would become close to a boss, but of all the guys from that mid-eighties L.A. Metro Group team, Chuck Pratt and I developed the strongest bond. He was a tough-as-nails law enforcement agent but also a very lovable man. Anyone who met him seemed to be taken by his warm personality. Over the years we became best friends—we went fishing together, and our wives and families hung out together. I spent much of my ATF career undercover, having limited contact with other agents over long periods of time, but Chuck was one of the guys I worked closely with. We did a big international armament caper in the mid-nineties, and he provided backup as I went undercover to bust a dealer trying to smuggle four artillery cannons into the country.

As Lanny, Allysson, and I entered the funeral home, I remembered the times during my Mongols case when Chuck had covered my ass. There was one especially scary day when I thought I might get ambushed and gunned down at the house of a gangster named Rocky. I can still remember the way Chuck covered me on Rocky's porch, his handgun drawn.

The Garcia Mortuary was packed with about ninety of Chuck's family, friends, and law enforcement brothers. Chuck's sudden passing had been a shock to us all. He'd gotten older and less agile but had always kept up his ex-marine workout regimen.

I'd been asked to give his eulogy. It took me a full minute to get my composure. I could see Chuck's twin sons in the front row, and just glancing at them started the tears streaming down my cheeks.

I started out by saying that Chuck had brought us all here for a reason. "I'm here not just to honor him and pay our respects," I said, "but so that we can all be together and see each other again, so that we can put our arms around each other and tell each other that we love one another. And we need to do that, because life is short, and we may not get another chance to do that. Less than a year ago I stood in front of this group and emceed Chuck's retirement, and it was a celebration. I can't believe I'm standing here today saying goodbye to my friend. I can't believe he was only given fifty-eight years to be with us."

I told a few stories about adventures that Chuck and I had had together. I told stories about the good times and the not so good times, about the times when we lived together and worked together on undercover capers and dangerous manhunts, like the one for Mark Stephens.

"Through it all, Chuck and I became best friends," I said. "And I loved him like he was my brother. I'll miss the good times with Chuck. I'll miss the security I felt when we worked together or were just hanging together for any reason. I'll miss the stories he used to tell, the friendship, the love. Most of all, I'll just miss my old friend forever."

When I finished speaking, I saw Lanny Royer wiping his face with the back of his hand. We gave each other a hug and then stood there, remembering our cases together. He ribbed me about how I'd nearly cost him his life on that mountaintop, not from the bullets flying in the dawn gunfight with Stephens but from the case of poison ivy that had sent him to the hospital.

It's something that's difficult to put into words, the degree of camaraderie and team spirit we'd all developed on that Stephens operation. When law enforcement people are involved in a heavy-duty case, there is such intense bonding that it goes above and beyond the brotherhood of the badge. It's an almost mystical connection that you share—and unless you were actually there, you'll never be part of it. The closest thing to this experience, I guess, is going into battle—and surviving the hell of warfare—together, as a unit.

It was well into the afternoon when we left the Garcia Mortuary. Lanny drove Allysson and me back to L.A., and I sat silently for most of the drive, ruminating for a long time about that group of guys—Chuck Pratt, Wayne Morrison, Lanny Royer, Howard Sanders, and Steve Kilgore—and about the bond we'd formed in the summer of '86, putting it all on the line to bring a gun-toting mountain man down from his hideout alive.

Acknowledgments

To my beautiful wife, for the inspiration and encouragement that she has provided, which has been the key to my success. I love you.

To Laura Ford, who has been much more than my editor at Random House. Your enthusiasm and friendship are cherished. Thanks, kiddo!

To the rest of the team at Random House, who have worked to make this book a success. Thank you so much.

To my partner, Doug Century. Thanks for all the hard work, my friend.

And finally, to Lanny Royer, Ken Cates, Howard Sanders, Steve

Kilgor, and Chuck Pratt, thanks for answering the call and standing with me in the face of danger. I will never forget.

—*William Queen*

I'd like to thank my parents, Jack and Marcia, and my daughter, Lena, for their constant support. I owe a special debt of gratitude to Sharon H. for helping me leap over a difficult hurdle in the revision process. And, of course, my deepest thanks to Bill Queen, a great partner and a one-of-a-kind lawman.

—*Douglas Century*

ABOUT THE AUTHORS

WILLIAM QUEEN is the author of the *New York Times* bestseller *Under and Alone*. He spent twenty years as a special agent with the U.S. Department of the Treasury, Bureau of Alcohol, Tobacco and Firearms. Queen is a Vietnam War veteran. He also served as an assistant operations and intelligence sergeant on a U.S. Army Special Forces A-Team and is a decorated soldier. Following his military service, Queen devoted his career to law enforcement, serving first as a local police officer and then as a U.S. Border Patrol agent before joining ATF. He is among the country's foremost experts on the violent world of outlaw motorcycle gangs and has lectured widely to law enforcement organizations in multiple countries. For his ground-breaking undercover work playing the part of biker "Billy St. John," William Queen was awarded the 2001 Federal Bar Association's Medal of Valor.

DOUGLAS CENTURY is the author of the critically acclaimed biography *Barney Ross* and the investigative memoir *Street Kingdom*, the co-author of the *New York Times* bestsellers *Under and Alone* and *Takedown*, and a frequent contributor to *The New York Times*. His nonfiction work has appeared in such publications as *Details*, *Rolling Stone*, *Men's Journal*, *New York*, *Vibe*, *Radar*, *Blender*, *Newsday*, and *The Guardian*. Century is a cum laude graduate of Princeton University. He lives in New York.

ABOUT THE TYPE

This book was set in Sabon, a typeface designed by the well-known German typographer Jan Tschichold (1902–74). Sabon's design is based upon the original letter forms of Claude Garamond and was created specifically to be used for three sources: foundry type for hand composition, Linotype, and Monotype. Tschichold named his typeface for the famous Frankfurt typefounder Jacques Sabon, who died in 1580.